Making
Regular
Schools
Special

Making Regular Schools Special

John Henderson

Chapter contributions by
Arthur Murphy, Esq.
Robert Mignone, M.D.

Foreword by Michael Jellinek, M.D.

Schocken Books · New York

First published by Schocken Books 1986
10 9 8 7 6 5 4 3 2 1   86 87 88 89
Copyright © 1986 by John Henderson

Library of Congress Cataloging-in-Publication Data
Henderson, John, 1929–
  Making regular schools special.
  Bibliography: p.
  Includes index.
  1. Handicapped children—Education—Law and
legislation—Massachusetts.   2. Handicapped children—
Education—Massachusetts.   I. Murphy, Arthur (Arthur J.)
II. Mignone, Robert.   III. Title.
KFM2795.9.H3H46   1986   344.744′0791   85–26147
                            347.4404791

Design by Thomas Nau
Manufactured in the United States of America
ISBN 0–8052–4008–X

To Matthew

Contents

Be ashamed to die until you have won some victory for humanity.

HORACE MANN, 1796–1859
Commencement Address,
Antioch College, 1859

Foreword

Providing the indicated range of services to an individual child is not a simple task. Extending such an effort to thousands of children with different needs, ages, and backgrounds is at times overwhelmingly complex. Chapter 766 is a commendable and impressive attempt to care for Massachusetts school children with special needs, but it implemented this delicate task using a blunt tool and broad strokes. The law established goals and a structural framework, but did not weave the many threads of diagnostic and educational special services into a workable fabric. The law provided no mechanisms to integrate necessary services and insufficient financial resources to meet the prescribed goals. The result has been less than adequate services and ongoing arguments that pass the fiscal "hot potato" among agencies that rationalize noninvolvement.

In order to appreciate the contribution of John Henderson's *Making Regular Schools Special,* it is first necessary to examine more closely the many threads of a special education system. The starting point is the child and an accurate assessment of the child's needs. The basic task of careful diagnosis is made quite difficult by a lack of qualified personnel and the broader limitations of what is known about child development and disorders. Deciding the nature of a child's difficulty often requires the thoughtful efforts of several professionals. Children do not present us with a well packaged and labeled diagnosis. As the child becomes more frustrated, a focal educational problem may soon lead to a general withdrawal from all subjects. For some children an educational problem becomes so overwhelming that psychological coping mechanisms break down. The child may become any combination of angry, hostile, disobedient, hyperactive, depressed, withdrawn, or negative. Thus a specific learning problem may be first detected as a behavioral issue or psychiatric disorder. Matters can become even more confusing. Wallerstein and Kelly in their prospective studies of children undergoing divorce have found that many six- to twelve-year-olds will react to the stress of the divorce with a decrease in school performance[1]. Thus, as we all have seen repeatedly, a problem in the emotional life of the family can dramatically affect the child's academic work. A further problem in the diagnostic process is that parents and teachers may see the same child differently. For example, studies of the Connors Questionnaire demonstrate that even on a relatively observable set of behaviors, such as Attention Deficit Disorder with Hyperactivity, parents' and teachers' rating scores show only a poor correlation[2].

If we move from the psychological perspective to purely educational diagnosis, matters only get worse. Despite the impressive advances in neuropsychological assessment, there is still no generally agreed upon classification system for learning disabilities. Numerous studies attempt to subdivide learning skills but few syndromes or distinctive diagnostic patterns emerge. Instead we tend to use jargon phrases like "processing" difficulties and offer very little in the way of specific treatments for specific disorders. Given the vast numbers of children receiving various remediation and "special" approaches to instruction, there is relatively little data to support the accuracy of diagnosis and efficacy of interventions. The final confounding variable is that children are not static but developing and evolving. Thus any plan requires careful review to determine whether it is still the appropriate approach.

The next thread that requires explanation is the family, with its own problems, traditions, and perspectives. Family assessment is especially difficult because parents may withdraw, or present a "packaged'" picture of their tensions and conflicts. Schools are in a peculiar position with regard to parents. Though professional and expert, teachers can be intimidated by hostile parents who feel their child is not getting the help he or she needs. Some parents undervalue education or, through neglect, are hardly involved in the school process. Others will withdraw or fight assistance because of guilt feelings, especially if the learning disabilities or handicaps follow a genetic pattern. Unfortunately the parental thread is further complicated by the 766 appeals process that pushes differences between parents and administration into a quasilegal battle over allocation of resources.

Parents of emotionally disturbed, learning impaired, or physically handicapped children suffer a repeated sense of loss and guilt. At each developmental point they must face again the realization that their child will not meet age appropriate goals whether in behavior, learning, or motor skills. These repeatedly forsaken hopes renew a sense of guilt that the parents are in some way to blame for their child's struggle and suffering. Sometimes this guilt and loss add dramatic intensity (sometimes successfully) to the demands for services—demands that highlight limitations and gaps brought about by inadequate funding.

The first phase of the weaving of these many threads requires a quality of team work that is well described in *Making Regular Schools Special*. Despite limitations in diagnostic and treatment information, the team serves as a focal point for various professional subspecialists to hammer out a treatment plan. The team must balance the various medical, parental, and educational perspectives and then forge a set of services that help the child and are consistent with local resources. In addition, despite the training and experience of the members, the team requires a leader with a broad background to assure that the final plan "makes sense," that is, fits the child's needs, is practical to implement, and is not so fragmented or confusing as to be counterproductive (for example, many different services at infrequent intervals which become disruptive to classroom participation). The team leader should not have a strong bias or self-interest: thus, a psychologist or social worker may offer more balance while a principle leading a team puts more emphasis on implementation within the school building.

Moving to the systems level for implementing a special needs program, a whole new set of threads must be integrated into the fabric. The local school district must organize a range of services that vary by goal and intensity. Decisions on how to cluster children must be made that are cost efficient but not detrimental to any one child. How does one divide into groups children with Attention Deficit Disorder, learning disabilities, and moderate behavior problems? What levels of disability or disorder should be together? What should one emphasize in children with multiple disorders? When dealing with multiply handicapped or retarded children, should there be mixed classes because some will have overlapping needs, or should children be transported longer distances to effect homogeneous groupings through consortia with other towns? When should expensive residential placements be started—early so as to have the least opportunity to effect changes (earlier discharge), or late as a money-saving last resort?

Beyond the school system there are the town, region, state, and federal governments. Although quite distant from the individual child, each level of government is involved in the service network. The town decides on the school budget and often elects a committee to decide how much to spend on special needs. The state sets standards and runs several large departments—for example, in Massachusetts: Public Health, Education, Mental Health, Social Service, correctional services, Commission for the Blind, etc. These agencies receive large state budgets and often have tendentious relationships with the school departments and with each other. Each bureaucracy has worked to shift cases and the resultant costs away from their own agency and to another. Each has levels of decisionmaking with the associated costs offset by the months or years of delay in implementing treatment plans. Only recently, more than a decade after the 766 law was passed, has there been a draft agreement to define and facilitate the cooperation of local schools and various state agencies in meeting the multiple needs of children and their familes.[3] This draft will be used on a pilot basis over the next school year and includes the following features: (1) limit time of decisionmaking; (2) foster interagency cooperation; (3) provide services in the least restrictive setting; (4) use the school team as the initial focal point of the evaluation and planning process; (5) add representatives to the team meeting of state agencies using the following criteria:

> In most cases the Chapter 766 Team Evaluation process should provide the forum for local cooperative planning around an individual child's program. Human service agencies' planning meetings (such as Department of Youth Services staffings) may be used, by agreement

of the parties, if it would be beneficial to the timely development of the child's program.

In the following instances, as soon as consent of the parent is received, a member of the appropriate agency(ies) will be invited to participate on or be a member of the Evaluation Team. The agency(ies) will make a commitment to ensure that a participant(s) is sent to the meeting.

1. A DMH area office caseworker will be invited if the child has received, is likely to need, or is in the process of seeking mental health, or mental retardation services from the Department of Mental Health or a local mental health clinic. Department of Mental Health participation will be subject to determination of eligibility for mental health or retardation services by a Department of Mental Health area office.

2. A Department of Social Services social worker, assigned educational advocate, foster parent, or other person with decision-making authority will be invited if the child is in the care or custody of the Department of Social Services and the parent does not retain rights to make decisions regarding the child's education.

3. A Department of Public Health case manager or family health services staff member will be invited if the child has received, has been determined eligible for, or is in the process of applying for any of the following services from the Department of Public Health: case management services for the multiply handicapped, Medical Review Team (intake for Pediatric Nursing Homes), or home health care services for medical needs. If the possible involvement of the Department of Public Health is not clear, the Family Health Services Coordinator at the appropriate Regional Health Office should be contacted to establish the family's status and the appopriate person to be invited.

4. A Department of Youth Services caseworker or Educational Liaison will be invited if the child has been committed to the Department of Youth Services (court adjudicated).

5. In accordance with the 1980 "Agreement Between the Massachusetts Rehabilitation Commission and the Department of Education," the assigned vocational rehabilitation counselor will be invited to participate in a special education evaluation in order to coordinate educational and vocational services if the adolescent is an applicant/client for Massachusetts Rehabilitation Services or appears to be potentially eligible for vocational rehabilitation services from the Commission. For young people with severe head injuries, the Massachusetts Rehabilitation Commission's Statewide Head Injury Program (SHIP) case worker will be contacted for determination of eligibility, participation

on the Evaluation Team, and assistance in case management and service provision.

6. In accordance with the "Agreement between the Massachusetts Commission for the Blind and the Massachusetts Department of Education Division of Special Education Regarding Services for Legally Blind and Visually Handicapped Children," the Massachusetts Commission for the Blind children's service workers will attend TEAM evaluation meetings as appropriate and indicated in the Massachusetts Commission for the Blind individual plans, or as requested by the family and/or school system. The Massachusetts Commission for the Blind can provide independent living social services and vocational rehabilitation services to eligible legally blind individuals. Some services are provided generally, when needed, to any eligible individual. Other services are provided only when the local school system is not mandated to provide them under Chapter 766.

The draft assures communication, coordinated services, and an overview case manager:

1. If a human service agency planning meeting is used as the individual planning conference, then the child's school district must be notified about the meeting as soon as possible. If the child has special education needs or is suspected of having special education needs and the individual plan may affect the child's educational placement under Chapter 766, then a representative from the local school district should be invited to the meeting. In all cases the school district should be informed of the outcome of the planning conference if the plan affects the child's education.

2. At the Team Evaluation Meeting the array of services available from the school department and the participating human service agency(ies) will be coordinated to ensure a program is developed in the least restrictive setting(s) appropriate to meet the child's needs. The Individualized Educational Plan, as well as agency service plans will be written to reflect the coordinated interagency services arrived at by the Evaluation Team in consultation with the Administrator of Special Education. Human service agency Individualized Service Plans or summaries will be attached to the Individualized Educational Plan.

a. Participating human service agencies will bring to the meeting all available, current and relevant assessments and/or any additional assessments to be determined in agreement with the Administrator of Special Education, subject to compliance with state and federal release of information requirements.

b. Case management responsibilities will be determined, by agreement of the Evaluation Team, to assure continuity and coordination of services between agencies and the school district.

The delicate issue of joint funding is addressed as follows:

1. If local school districts and human service agencies agree on the education and service plans, but cannot identify appropriate or available programs or services, or adequate funding is not available at the human service agency area level, then the agency and Administrator of Special Education shall initiate appropriate intra-agency procedures to locate necessary programs, services or funding.

2. If agencies and local school districts agree that they have some responsibility for the child, but cannot agree on a description of the child's educational and human service needs, and/or an appropriate educational/service plan to meet those needs, then:

a. The human service agencies and school districts identified as having responsibility for the student will each develop a service plan that will be shared with the other participants. A meeting will be held within ten working days of the Team Evaluation meeting to review the service and educational plans and to resolve the gaps in service that appear in the coordination of service and educational plans. A Department of Education Special Education Mediator and an Office for Children Advocate will serve to mediate the differences between the plans and to help the agencies arrive at an agreement on the delivery of services. All agency plans will be amended to reflect the mediated agreement, and will be implemented as soon as they are accepted by the parents, guardian, or child over 18.

b. If an agreement cannot be reached, then the participants of this meeting shall write and implement an interim plan that will cover the maximum period of six months. Services will begin within five working days of acceptance of the interim plan by the parent or guardian.

In addition mediation procedures are outlined if agencies cannot agree upon a cost-sharing approach.

The draft agreement also attempts to deal with the most hotly contested cost-sharing decisions, namely, the child's need for residential services:

1. When an EOHS Agency determines that a child must be cared for in a residential school program, and a Team Evaluation determines that a child may be educated in a day component of a residential school program, then the human service agency(ies) and the school district shall cost share the residential placement. These costs shall be shared in the following manner:

a. For placements at residential schools which have both a day rate and a residential rate established by the Rate Setting Commission, the school district shall be responsible to pay the day rate and the human service agency shall be responsible to pay the difference between the day rate and the full residential/instructional rate.

b. For placements at residential schools which do not have a day rate established by the Rate Setting Commission, the cost of the placement shall be shared on a 50/50 basis between the school district and the human service agency. If more than one human service agency is involved, the costs will be shared equally by all agencies involved.

However the document does not address fully how to resolve differences between agencies in cost-sharing residential placements and depends heavily on this process occurring at a bureaucratic distance from the local school board and region.

Although this draft agreement, if formally adopted, will represent a major breakthrough, there is still much left to local cooperation for design and too little authorized to fund implementation. John Henderson's Project Link described in this book has anticipated both the working agreement (although the book was completed well before the draft was issued) and a rational method to make the agreement benefit the needs of children. Project Link provides a forum for interagency discussion and a model to provide more regional control of decisionmaking and funds. Rather than the team's plans having to be reviewed by bureaucrats at multiple levels in each of the collaborating agencies, Project Link provides funds based on the decisions of those who know the child rather than on a paper review.

Making Regular Schools Special is a history of special educational services in Massachusetts and a broadly applicable manual for meeting the needs of children in any school district. The experience in Massachusetts suggests that moving from design goals and threads to a finished, usable fabric is a slow, complex, and highly political process.

Despite every effort at careful team diagnostic planning and interagency collaboration, the ultimate quality and durability of the fabric will depend on the value our society places on children. Currently the prognosis is poor. Federal cutbacks have hurt many medical, social, and educational programs for children. Elected officials are well aware that children don't vote. Therefore funds move toward the elderly with Social Security protected while educational programs and Medicaid for children are cut. On a state level, a bill limiting town property taxes is hailed as a success because police and fire protection survived the cuts; however, there is little mention that this law resulted in major cuts in school district educational budgets. John Henderson's goal in *Making Regular Schools Special* requires first that society consider children special, support that decision with money, and then implement that commitment by carefully weaving a fabric of services that have a demonstrable benefit for children with special needs.

MICHAEL JELLINEK, M.D.
Chief, Child Psychiatry Service,
Massachusetts General Hospital
Assistant Professor of Psychiatry
(Pediatrics), Harvard Medical School

1. Judith S. Wallerstein and Joan B. Kelly, *Surviving the Breakup: How Children and Parents Cope with Divorce* (New York: Basic Books, 1980).
2. E. Taylor, "Syndromes of overactivity and attention deficit," in *Child Psychiatry: Modern Approaches,* ed. Michael Rutter and Lionel Hersov, 2nd ed. (London: Blackwell Scientific Publications, 1985), 424–43.
3. Draft: Interim Agreement on Interagency Coordination for School-Age Children in Massachusetts (Boston, Mass.: Executive Office of Human Services, 1985).

Preface

In 1972 a new law was passed by the Great and General Court of the Commonwealth of Massachusetts, entitled Public Law 766. The chapter heading for the law describes it as "An Act further regulating programs for children requiring special education and providing reimbursement therefor." In passing this public law, the state legislative body had guaranteed free and public education for all of the Commonwealth of Massachusetts' handicapped and learning disabled children between the ages of three and twenty-one.

The passage of Public Law 766 has greatly changed the lives of these special-needs children. For many of them it has meant leaving institutions, returning to their home communities, and entering the public schools for the first time. With this change came the opportunity for new achievement and growth, thanks to individual education plans that aimed at developing areas of strength around their limitations. Moreover, moving these youngsters into the public schools left the institutions free to fill an important support role in the communities.

The law also brought about a great change in my own life. It meant leaving a relatively easy job as principal of a seven-hundred-pupil elementary school in Connecticut to take up the often perplexing but always challenging study of child psychology and learning disabilities. As an associates candidate at the Institute of Education, London University, England, I conducted research into the current status of special education and found that the Scandinavian countries were at least ten years in advance of Great Britain and the United States. The study of the Scandinavian method was to influence me greatly when I later came to set up my own special-education program for a public school system in Massachusetts.

I write about special education as I have known it. If at times I am critical of a bureau or an agency, it is because I am speaking from my own experience. My comments about the Office for Children, for example, should in no way be construed as a dismissal of the concept of having advocates for children. I am, however, critical of the lack of training and experience that these advocates were given prior to being placed in the field.

Fieldstone Farm
Essex, Massachusetts

Acknowledgments

I would like to thank my wife, Valerie, for her support and help during the two and a half years it took to write this book. I would also like to acknowledge the contributions given to me by colleagues of my school department, especially Gail Macklem and Faith Conrad, who through their work made a direct contribution to the book. I owe a special debt to members of Governor Dukakis's Committee on Education and to members of the Massachusetts State House Library staff who willingly made documents available to me.

Introduction

Public Law 766 has upgraded special education significantly in the Commonwealth of Massachusetts. It has given needed structure to special education. It has allowed those of us who care about the field to build up a delivery system with specialists and programs that surpass any others in the country—a system that has been used as a model for Federal Law 94-142, mandating comprehensive special-education programs for all states, at a standard to match that of Massachusetts.

Making Regular Schools Special contains ten chapters, seven written by me and three by professional colleagues with whom I have worked closely for the past ten years as I have developed a special-education delivery system. Arthur Murphy is an attorney who has put his knowledge of the law toward helping schools sort out the complex problems and disagreements with parents over the delivery of services for children. He has worked closely with me in mediating dozens of cases. He has always sought out solutions with the best interests of the children in mind. Robert Mignone is a wonderfully versatile and pragmatic psychiatrist who takes a holistic approach toward the child and who always makes teachers and specialists with whom he works feel important and valued members of the team. Mr. Murphy's two chapters deal with the appeals process and issues within the current educational law; Dr. Mignone's chapter addresses the role of the consultant psychiatrist in the schools. My seven chapters offer the parent, special educator, politician, and human service provider a comprehensive picture of the component parts of the special-education delivery system, its programs, its staffing patterns, the dynamics of its team structure, as well as a knowledge of those departments and agencies with whom the public, special educators, and teams become involved.

Chapter 8 is a very special chapter for me, for it is on these pages that the transcript of an entire appeals case is brought to life in *Matthew* v. *a School System in Massachusetts*. Matthew is a ten-year-old Down's syndrome child, whose parents wanted him to receive his education in his home school with the least restrictive delivery system possible. This would have required a fully qualified teacher. The position of the superintendent of schools was that an aide rather than a teacher was adequate to meet Matt's needs and that service-delivery team should seek placement for Matt outside the home school. This position prompted Matt's parents to reject his educational plan and bring the case before a hearing officer. The team agreed with the parents. As you read the testimony, you will understand why team members must be specialists who are well trained and well grounded in group dynamics.

My purpose in writing *Making Regular Schools Special* is to highlight how important it is for all our states to implement special-education programs and to reaffirm the importance of Public Law 766. After a decade of involvement in Massachusetts, I feel it is time for us to assess our accomplishments in the field and to make the necessary adjustments in our delivery system so as to ensure that the learning disabled and handicapped receive the high standard of education and support they deserve.

Making
Regular
Schools
Special

1

The Shaping
of a Special-Educator

A little over fifteen years ago I turned my interests toward developmental psychology and the special education of handicapped children. As the principal of a seven-hundred-pupil elementary school in Connecticut, I was fortunate to have on my staff a school psychologist and a consulting psychiatrist. I say "fortunate" because fifteen years ago at the elementary-school level this was the exception rather than the rule. At that time no satisfactory internal structure was defined in school programs for the utilization of such professionals. We worked closely together to establish such a structure, and I perceived what an important role developmental psychology could and should play in school programs.

These were eventful years. Our town was one of the first school systems in New England to be federally funded for busing. In 1966 a team of public school officials joined forces to develop and implement a plan to integrate twenty-seven black and Puerto Rican kindergartners, first-graders, and second-graders into my school's regular classroom programs. One of the prime movers of this project was Dr. Ira Singer, then an assistant superintendent of schools. These children all came from the city ghettos to our suburban school. Watching them thrive in their new setting over a period of six years convinced me that environment played a dominant role over heredity in their development. Of course, the transition time was not an easy one for any of us. Problems did arise, and many questions were asked by teachers. Our plan called for our professional psychological staff to be readily avail-

3

able to teachers so that solutions to these problems could be worked out on a day-to-day basis. Because the teachers felt supported, they were able to develop a caring and nurturing climate in which the youngsters could realize social, emotional, and educational growth to their full potential. Three-quarters of these children completed their education in our school and went on to junior high school.

At the same time all of this was happening, one of my administrative responsibilities was to evaluate the progress of handicapped children who had been assigned to segregated programs outside our school. During my visits to these programs, it became evident that the desired social, emotional, and educational growth was *not* taking place. Inevitably, the comparison was presented to me. The bused children flourished in their new environment. Why should the handicapped children continue to languish in programs segregated from their regular home schools?

Several years into the implementation of the busing program, I decided to train in the fields of clinical and developmental psychology. I took night courses at our local university and enrolled in two successive summer programs. By this time I was thoroughly caught up in the idea of a new career in special education, and I applied for and was awarded sabbatical leave. With three-quarters of my formal coursework done toward a qualification of school psychologist, I left for England to complete my study and to participate in a work experience. I had been accepted by London University in its associateship program.[1] I was very fortunate because, up to this point, the university had been adhering strictly to a Freudian approach to psychology, which would have been very limiting for me; now, however, it had turned to an eclectic approach to developmental psychology, which was to prove far more valuable for my purposes.

An associate program at the university could be hand-tailored to meet the needs of the participants. I organized my year around study, working as a school psychologist for Kent County Council, and spending one afternoon a week as an intern at Queen Elizabeth's Hospital for Children, London, and one evening a week at Off Centre, an adolescent drop-in center in London.[2] It was a busy schedule, and after Christmas, with most of my formal coursework completed, I settled down to a school psychologist's job for three days a week.

As a school psychologist in Kent, I was assigned a caseload of over eighty students spread over literally dozens of towns and two cities in South Kent. The total school population in my assigned area was 66,000, and the recommended ratio of psychologist to children was one to 10,000. This was not an unusual situation for a psychologist in England to be in.

The established procedure there was to refer children to remedial centers, often at a considerable distance from the schools, and these centers made no attempt to involve the child's school in either initial assessment or follow-up. A second alternative was to certify the child as being "educationally subnormal." This automatically removed the child from school and placed him or her in either a residential or a day program in a county-supported institution. I tried to show teachers in the classroom how to assess the nature of children's handicaps and suggested appropriate teaching strategies and curriculum materials to help the children to be successful in school. The sheer number of referrals I received made it impossible for me to make any real impact, but the response from the few teachers I was able to help was appreciative. I could see that the frustration the teachers felt because of their isolation was partly alleviated by these efforts.

However, I, too, was frustrated by my attempts to make an inroad into a system that I felt was not optimally organized to assist the handicapped and learning-disabled child. In fact, the United Kingdom's comprehensive "White Paper on Special Education"[3] did not come out until May of 1978, and only then was a continuum of special-educational needs, rather than discrete categories of handicaps, established. New priorities were set, including children with significant learning disabilities and behavioral disorders as well as those with disabilities of mind and body. At least by this time there was a recommendation for establishing a more realistic ratio of psychologist to children. On my return after the first semester to London University, I began to research what was happening elsewhere in Europe and was encouraged when I discovered the system that had been planned and was now partially implemented in Scandinavia.

The Scandinavian Model

A study entitled "Making Ordinary Schools Special" had just been completed in 1972 by the College of Special Education, London University, reporting on the integration of physically handicapped and learning-disabled children in Scandinavian schools.[4] In Sweden it reported that in 1967–68, out of a total of nearly 900,000 children in ordinary schools, there were 38,120 children in 3,720 special classes, and almost as many (29,300 in 1965–66) in ordinary classes receiving supplementary lessons. These figures give us a picture of where the Swedes started just under twenty years ago when they launched their program to turn ordinary schools into special schools. Their National Board of Education states that its aim is to present a flexible system of possibilities, enabling parents and children to choose between alternatives and making every effort to find out what is best for the individual child and his or her development. The three major alternatives are as follows: (1) The child attends school in an ordinary class with remedial teaching where necessary, technical aids, transport to and from school, and personal assistance. (2) The child attends a special class for the motor-handicapped within the ordinary school, with additional remedial teaching, personal assistance, and treatment facilities, and lives either at home or in a hostel for motor-handicapped pupils. (3)The child receives schooling, medical care, and so on, and boarding facilities if necessary, in an institution for the motor-handicapped. In order to implement this system, plans were made to decentralize the country's delivery system and place the bulk of personnel out in the regular schools. Those responsible for the reorganization drew up standards for school buildings that had to be met before the handicapped could be moved in. They worked out a special transportation system and began teacher-training programs at the regular schools. At the time of the report (1972), impressive numbers of special-needs children had been integrated into the regular schools—and, on balance, with great success. The report candidly states that where these efforts met with administrative resistance from a school principal, little true integration took place;

but these situations were definitely the exception rather than the rule. The team concept for service delivery was the chosen model. The team consisted of a school psychologist, a social worker, a speech therapist, and three to five consultant teachers, including one preschool teacher with experience in working with varying types of handicaps. The team members, it was planned, would go out from centers to the ordinary schools and special classes to give direct service to students and to serve as consultants. The teams were assigned pediatricians who were shared among several centers.

In Scandinavia there appeared to be more awareness of the need to give the nonhandicapped pupils, their teachers, and their parents information about the handicapped children than there was in the United States and elsewhere. It was recognized that getting information to the right people could significantly affect the academic success and, even more, the social adjustment of the handicapped group. Although little research has been done in this important area, the empirical evidence suggests that careful preparation in the ordinary classes can do much to minimize the problem of teasing and, to a lesser extent, of social isolation.

Let me describe several illustrations of what is being done. In one Swedish secondary school (for ages thirteen to fifteen), where there are three classes for severely handicapped pupils, the head of the school holds a special assembly for all the new children. He calls the register so that the children are aware from the start that there are handicapped children among them, but since this first encounter is in the presence of a calm adult, the nonhandicapped group is given some cues about how to treat the other children. The classes then leave the hall, the handicapped group going out first, and the head then tells the other children a little about them. At the end of the first or during the second year, the children are shown a film about cerebral palsy (CP). (The handicapped children are consulted on this and asked if they wish to be present when the film is shown, which they have always chosen to do.) At this school the problem of teasing has not arisen.

Another encouraging example comes from a town in central Sweden where "cerebral palsy" was widely used as a term of mockery in all schools. One of the special-class teachers prepared, with the CP children, a tape that had a simple medical introduction and then recorded the CP children explaining how they did certain things, why their behavior might sometimes seem odd, and how it felt to be spastic. This tape was sent around to all the schools in the district, with the teachers giving time for discussion, and a great improvement in attitude was reported.

Another common practice is for teachers in special classes (whether for physically handicapped, hearing-impaired, or speech-retarded children) to go around to the ordinary classes with some of the special equipment, such as deaf aids, explaining the difficulties of the handicapped pupils and how the equipment helps them. In several cases children in ordinary classes have been taken around to the special classes and treatment rooms, where it is explained to them what goes on there and where the use of the equipment is demonstrated to them. These methods are probably more effective than simply getting the ordinary class teachers to talk to their pupils.

It has also been found advisable to give the nonhandicapped children's parents information about the handicapped children, partly as a matter of public education and partly so that they can answer their own children's questions correctly without perpetuating mistaken beliefs. In one school all new parents are invited to visit the school, and the head, while taking them around, explains as a matter of course the purpose of the ramps and elevator, and so can introduce the special classes in a natural way. In other cases experts from special schools and hospitals are called in to speak at parents' meetings.

Various methods are used to inform the members of the regular staff about the physically handicapped groups' problems. In one school a pediatrician comes in to talk to all teachers and assistants who will be involved with these children, and to any others interested. In other schools this function is carried out by the special-class teachers. The Swedish National Board of Education also tries to keep ordinary teachers informed, by means of booklets distributed to most schools, about how they can help handicapped children in their classes. The climate of public opinion in Scandinavia, particularly in Sweden, aided by the press and television and by a strong Association of Parents of Handicapped Children, tends to encourage teachers to take a positive attitude toward having handicapped children in ordinary schools.

The report on the Scandinavian system concludes by saying that once the community has been sensitized to the needs of the handicapped and has given its cooperation in turning ordinary schools into special schools, there still remains the very real possibility that a child may need care and/or treatment outside the community, and this is a contingency for which there is need for planning.

Observing the progress that had already been made in Scandinavia, along with my working experience in hospitals, schools, and clinics in England, convinced me that some major changes must take place in the education of the learning disabled and handicapped child in the United States. It seemed providential that upon my return to the States in 1972, state legislation covering special education had just been written in Massachusetts, and was to be followed by federal legislation in 1977.

2
Launching a New Program

On my return to the United States, I accepted the job of director of special education in a Massachusetts school district with school population of 2,500 housed in six school buildings. To be able to work within the framework of Public Law 766, though it was a loosely defined law, was more than I had dared to hope while I was formulating my plans in England.

The first year in Massachusetts found me wrestling with budgetary problems, selling a special-education system of delivery to the community, interviewing and hiring staff, and implementing the plan. Our plan called for Building Planning and Placement Teams to be set up in each of the six school buildings in the school district. Each team was to have a school psychologist as chairperson who reported directly to me as director. The teams consisted of the school psychologist, who chaired the child study teams and gave direct service to students and consultation to staff; a speech pathologist shared between two buildings; a learning disabilities specialist; a school nurse shared between two buildings; an administrator; a classroom teacher; and parents. In addition, there were the part-time support services of an occupational and a physical therapist and consultants available for the blind, deaf, and any other types of handicaps that presented themselves to the team. We were also very fortunate to be able to draw on the expertise of a consulting psychiatrist (Robert Mignone, the author of Chapter 5 of this book). We decided that he should function as an integral part of the team structure and should be available to teams and the teachers for consultation, and that he would observe students in classrooms, consult with parents, and assist us in questions of a medical nature. In England, I had observed that psychiatrists kept themselves apart from the schools, secluding themselves in clinics and hospitals. Our model was different, for the psychiatrist enjoyed an equal membership on the working team. Our team psychologists, when assessing children at hospitals, would be joined by a staff clinician, recommended by our psychiatrist, and together they would conduct the testing. This way we expanded our knowledge, so that the next time we were called upon to do outside assessments, we could go on our own. This proved to be one of the best in-service techniques we employed. We budgeted monies to pay for second opinions from hospitals and clinics so that we could benefit from new insights into some of the more perplexing cases that were presented to us. By gathering such data and sharing them with parents, we were far more likely to convince families that schools were truly their advocates—that we and they shared the common goal of wanting to get at the root of the problem and solve it.

Working as a Team

For us, the team process started when a teacher, a parent, a student over eighteen, a doctor, or a clinic referred a child for a known or suspected handicap or disability that seemed to be getting in the way of learning and/or social development. The first kind of assistance offered by the team was consultation. For instance, a teacher who was concerned about a child's progress would approach the team to discuss the problem. If the problem had substance, a written prereferral plan was worked out. Then, after a thirty-day trial period, the team might agree that a referral was necessary. If this was the case, a full assessment plan was prepared and carried out. The team members then met again and designed a written individual education plan, following their mandate that the least restrictive program must be sought and carried out in their own school. As in the Scandinavian system, we recognized the need for possible hospital and private school placements in certain cases. However, our own options ranged from minimal support to the student and teacher, with the student doing virtually all his or her work in the regular classroom, to special support programs conducted in the school, removing the students for substantial periods from the mainstream of the regular school programs, yet always working toward reentry into the regular program. Our counseling support programs frequently involved mixed groups of handicapped students who were adjusting well to school and those who were having difficulty. Individual therapy—speech, physical, or occupational—was conducted during times that were least disruptive to the student's academic program.

One challenge we faced was to be sure we gave the children the correct amount of support. If we accepted children just because the teachers or parents wanted to avoid their own responsibility, we would be doing a disservice to all concerned and would be creating a logjam of referrals. On the other hand, if the teacher or parent needed to understand how to apply some behavior management techniques at home or in the classroom, it was important that our team come forward with the necessary instruction and support. We found that the children who needed substantially separate programs conducted in our learning centers also often needed a counseling component for themselves and their families. To meet these needs, we organized an outreach counseling program housed in our high school. Families could request this service through their Building Team and were encouraged to elect their option of having the school psychologist share all assessment work with their outreach counselor and keep in constant communication with the counselor regarding the child's progress in his or her school program. This proved to be one of the most difficult programs to set up, as we had to negotiate for these services through the Department of Mental Health.

Working with Advocacy Groups and Parents

Community supporters for Chapter 766 were everywhere. What with parent advocacy groups and child advocates supplied to parents from our state-run Office for Children,[1] parents who once (and I think justifiably) felt that schools had ignored the handicapped, now had the upper hand, thanks to the law. And how some of them did abuse it! The challenge as we saw it was not how to get advocacy for our new special-education programs, but rather how to channel this surge of parental energy that seemed fueled by indignation over past injustices, real and imagined, inflicted upon the handicapped by the public schools. If we were not careful, we feared, we administrators would soon be portrayed as opponents of special education as we tried tirelessly to administer a complex and often poorly defined public law. A knowledgeable, wealthy family bound and determined to get their private school bills paid would instruct their lawyer not to spare the whip when push came to shove at an appeals hearing. Child advocates frequently assured parents that it was standard procedure to secure a second opinion from a private team of clinical specialists first and then send the bill to the schools.

I hasten to note, as a supporter of Public Law 766, that the Office for Children, which supplied these advocates to parents, existed before the 766 legislation was implemented. The organization's role was ill-defined from the start. Its advocate staff was for the most part young and inexperienced and in most cases poorly trained. A better training program for advocates would go a long way toward achieving a better balance of power for families and schools. A well-trained staff could play a useful role as advocates for children.

The law also mandated that every school system have a parent support group, and ours was to be very different from any we have known then or now. Ours was formed as a task-oriented group. That is, projects were to be agreed upon that would support the development of our programs; and the role of parent participants was to be clearly outlined; and tangible, achievable goals were to be set. The best way, I think, to give a sense of how our parent advocacy group functioned is to describe some of the projects it undertook with us.

Summer vacation was a problem time for the handicapped in our towns. Eight children really needed an ongoing program twelve months of the year, but alas, the public law did not provide any funds beyond the nine-month regular school year. Our task became that of setting up a summer program to fill this void. Our chairperson put together a subcommittee whose goal we clearly outlined. We met with the town's parks and recreation director and worked out a model plan whereby the town would include the handicapped in its already existing recreation program. We needed a certified, qualified swimming instructor and special swimming pool time. We needed aides to supervise the handicapped in their crafts program and during lunchtime. If we could get these needs approved by the town officials, my department would guarantee that physical and occupational therapy, counseling, and speech therapy continue during the summer. We presented this plan to the town selectmen, and were delighted when they agreed to cooperate. We had even found a way whereby the town could be reimbursed for half of the program costs. After one successful summer of activities and therapies, the parents and I presented our accomplishments to our school committee. They were visibly pleased, for, instead of a group of unruly parents shouting their demands, as many towns were experiencing, they had witnessed a support group that had proudly completed a task.

As the saying goes, nothing succeeds like success, and with our first task completed, we went ahead and formed a second committee to act as a support force for a group home for mentally retarded young adults. This project took a great deal of commitment and time. The committee saw the work through to the very end and served long enough in board of directors roles to set standards for our new home and others that we planned. One of the latest and most important parent projects is the Therapeutic Equitation Program, in Boxford, Massachusetts. Marjorie Kittredge, a local resident and a fine horsewoman, developed this program, which uses horseback riding as therapy for handicapped children. As the program's head instructor puts it, it is a great accomplishment for a little person to be able to make a big horse do what he or she wants. Each child's program is individually planned and carefully follows a logical step-by-step process, moving through care of the animal, care of tack, exercises, and horsemanship. Similar programs have been conducted in England, and the reports of doctors enthusiastically supported this form of therapy for the promotion of both psychological and physical growth.

Working with Children: Four Cases

In order to convey the complexity of some of the cases that we have worked with, I wish to discuss four examples. In each case, names and settings have been altered.

Colin

Our team first met Colin at a children's hospital in Boston. Then ten years old, he used a wheelchair because he had become paralyzed as a result of an automobile accident. Our school team—a psychologist, a speech pathologist, learning-disabilities specialists, and myself—arrived at the hospital and found Colin in the hall outside his room. Colin's mother and a nurse were there as well, and as we gathered around him, it was a little crowded and awkward in the hospital corridor. We had, of course, come to meet Colin, but also to attend a hospital staffing session, which had been scheduled for 10 A.M. As it was getting close to that hour, we said goodbye to Colin, and he gave us a sort of lopsided smile—he had lost his speech owing to the paralysis of his face. We filed into the conference room, which was already filling up with hospital staff. Settling ourselves around the table, we saw about us a comprehensive medical staff headed by Colin's doctor. After introductions, the doctor presented us with Colin's case summary, as follows.

Colin was a nine-year-old boy referred for in-patient psychological evaluation as part of medical admission. He was transferred from a nearby hospital where he had received intensive rehabilitation following a head injury. Because of his accident he had sustained an immediate right hemiplegia and remained in a coma for ten days. A left temple decompression was performed, with findings of contused, swollen, and seminecrotic brain tissue, a small amount of which was removed. A left ventricular peritoneal shunt was inserted, and Colin showed rapid improvement. He had been receiving and would continue to receive speech, occupational, and physical therapy. A brief review of the developmental history revealed progress within normal limits. Before the accident, Colin had been an excellent student in school.

This report was the first we had received, and its presentation came midway in Colin's one-year period of hospitalization. The staff psychologist reported next. She told us that testing of Colin in his bed and in his wheelchair yielded evidence of right hemiplegia as well as poor hand and trunk control. He was able to communicate by using his left hand for sign language and finger spelling. At the time of testing he had begun to phonate minimally and was able to repeat single syllables. In his interaction he was friendly to the examiner and was able to relate what had happened to him, and he demonstrated appropriately sad affect when speaking about family and friends. It appeared that he was very much in touch with his feelings and responded to an opportunity to share them with someone. It was noted that he tired easily, which necessitated numerous testing situations.

In summary, we were told by the psychologist that Colin was functioning within the average range of intelligence, which represented a considerable loss from the high range he had demonstrated before the accident.

It was indicated to us that Colin should continue to be involved in the various therapies. It was felt that he could benefit from psychotherapy to help him through the recovery period and adjustment to his handicap. Colin was to be enrolled in the hospital's education program. We did not know at this point when he would be able to return to our school, but, as it turned out, just six months from this visit our local newspaper ran a feature story about Colin's miraculous recovery and return to public school with a special-needs support system under Public Law 766.

During Colin's year in the hospital, our team had been able to prepare for his eventual return. Teachers at the school were shown the hospital reports encouragingly describing his continuing progress. They knew of the seriousness of his condition, and we helped them to understand the problems accompanying his nonambulatory condition, and explained how his speech, though much improved, would be hard to understand at first. His left side, leg, arm, and hand had only just begun to show signs of some dexterity returning. Although his visual acuity was unaffected, his peripheral vision was limited. His amnesia was essentially improved.

The psychologist and principal worked together to determine which teachers Colin would have in fifth grade. Once this was done, the psychologist worked with the students who were to be Colin's classmates, so as to gain their support and understanding of his needs. Several members of the team then screened and interviewed candidates for the position of aide to assist Colin in getting about, toileting, dressing, and undressing. We were confident that we had thought of everything we could do to prepare for Colin's return to school. The hardest thing, we knew, would be to avoid spoiling the boy. We knew that Colin's growth in school, both academically and socially, was to a large measure dependent upon his desire to become an independent person again. We discussed this issue with Colin's aide because it was he who would be most consistently at the boy's side.

When Colin arrived, he was warmly greeted by classmates and school professionals. His first day was to set the pattern for the many days to come. He arrived at school by taxi, strapped in by a safety belt, and was helped by his aide into his wheelchair. His school day opened with homeroom exercises, followed by reading class, then a session of occupational therapy, math class followed by speech therapy, lunch, social studies and science, and a physical therapy session at home. Once a week Colin had a session with the school psychologist. This was followed up by monthly meetings with Colin's mother.

For the first two years things went very well, and it was a joy to see Colin's classmates rush out to greet his taxi and clamor about him, competing over whose turn it was to push the wheelchair into school. By the end of the third year, you would not have recognized Colin. All but one of the therapists were delighted with his progress, his speech had greatly improved, he was walking with the aid of a cane, he remembered past events, and academically he was at or above grade level. The school psychologist, however, was very concerned. She had had lengthy discussions with the team's consulting psychiatrist to share the results of psychological testing, which had turned up some signs of compulsive thinking and anxiety on Colin's part as well as feelings of inadequacy centered on issues of rejection by peers. Colin's responses on projective tests showed that he clearly perceived his family as displaying aggressive feelings toward him. He felt rejected, experienced the world as a dangerous place, and saw home as a less than understanding place. To a large extent this composite picture told us what Colin was thinking and how he was feeling.

Our task now was to decide what we could do to help. In school Colin had developed some maladaptive behavior that was beginning to turn classmates against him. It seemed that he would do almost anything to gain attention, even trying to trip people up with his cane. Problems at home were reported at parent conferences. These behaviors went on for some time and seemed to be getting worse. The team met frequently, and from these deliberations came a plan to include family counseling. Counseling goals were written and included in the individualized educational plan. The team also thought it was necessary to control the academic environment. They arranged for Colin to have fewer teachers each day. His program became more self-contained.

Follow-up testing six months later began to show the positive effects of these plan revisions. At the time of writing this report, Colin has one more year before graduating high school. We have just added Therapeutic Equitation to his program, with built-in goals for physical therapy and emotional development. The team feels Colin will make it. Neither he nor the team has had an easy time. There have been setbacks, but on balance, significant gains have been realized. To us this is a testimony to a support system rooted in the public schools, which is far superior to the alternatives that would have faced Colin if he had remained in a hospital or been placed in a residential school.

Jeff

The next case clearly points up the importance of having a psychiatrist on staff, for the solution to this student's difficulties turned out to have its ideology in the medical realm. Jeff was referred by his classroom teacher because of low academic achievement and erratic acting-out behavior. At one moment he seemed to be introverted, at the next he seemed unable to control himself. Our learning-disabilities specialist reported that Jeff, a fourth-grader, was very difficult to test. One day he was cooperative, and the next day he hid under the table and later ran wildly around the room. Patience on the part of the examiner enabled her to determine that Jeff was two years below age level norms in auditory memory and as much as four years below age level norms in certain other tasks. Visual–motor integration skills were three years delayed. The examiner observed difficulty with handwriting and math computation. The school psychologist gave a lengthy account of Jeff's family history and then went on to report that his intelligence fell within the normal range. She identified weaknesses in attention and concentration and in visual–motor integration. The composite picture clearly indicated that the case should be reviewed by the team psychiatrist.

The psychiatrist met with both Jeff and his parents and recommended that they have the family pediatrician review all our findings to the possible end that medication might be used as a control for hyperactivity.[2] Such medication, he said, might allow Jeff to attend better to his schoolwork. The family doctor was contacted by the parents in this case and, after consultation with the psychiatrist, decided to prescribe Ritalin.[3] He asked the school team to report to him weekly about Jeff's behavior during the trial period of the medication.

This case was a success story. However, the team concluded that not all hyperactive children in our experience respond as well as Jeff did, and it is important to remember that medication in and of itself does not bring about learning but only slows down the metabolism, making it possible for the teaching–learning act to take place.

Kate

The third case is that of six-and-a-half-year-old Kate, who came to us with a medical diagnosis as a cerebral palsied, spastic, quadriplegic child with a history of grand mal seizures. Kate was our second nonambulatory, nonverbal student, and along with our excitement at having her join us came a certain amount of apprehension. We met Kate for the first time in September just before the opening of school. Her parents had brought her to school so that the team could start a series of assessments before school started. It took us about two weeks to complete our tests and put together a composite picture of Kate as we saw her and then to develop her program. The team requested that I attend all their sessions, and I saw the following picture emerge.

The psychologist saw Kate as an engaging, socially responsive, nonverbal child. Her eyes followed others' bodily movements, and she responded appropriately to conversation by displaying expressions of shyness and pleasure. Kate was found to be functioning in the average to low-average range of intelligence. The psychologist recommended that family counseling be included in Kate's program. The speech pathologist recommended that the Blissymbolics communication system become Kate's chief means of communicating to the outside world. The occupational therapist recommended three and a half hours of therapy per week, with emphasis on a feeding program, developing arm–hand functions, toilet training, and general body exercises to relieve fatigue and develop muscle tone. We hired a full-time aide for Kate who worked with the learning-disabilities specialist to deliver her program. Kate was with us only a short time, and her program undoubtedly needed many adjustments before she graduated from high school.

Mark

The last case to be reported is a sad one, for we watched a first-grade child slowly lose his sight over a four-year period and at the same time saw his suffering caused by juvenile rheumatoid arthritis. The blindness and the arthritis, the doctors told us, were directly related. Mark became our first totally blind child. We had others who were designated as legally blind or partially sighted but no one who suffered both total loss of sight and crippling arthritis.

Mark's special support system consisted of counseling from the school psychologist, work with a teacher of the blind trained at the master's level in the teaching of braille, and mobility training. The teacher ran a program to help the regular teachers and children at Mark's school understand what it was like for a blind child to go to a regular school. I attended one of these sessions and was fascinated to watch as the children were asked to look through wax paper at the print in a book to see what it was like to be partially sighted. They were also asked to peer through a cardboard cylinder in search of a penny that had been thrown on the floor to demonstrate the difficulties of limited peripheral vision. Then came the blindfolding of a child and the assigning of another to be his or her guide. These activities were well received by the children, and they seemed eager to be able to assist Mark whenever they could in class or in the playground. Mark functioned in the classroom totally independently of the outside support that I have outlined. He moved between classroom and cafeteria on his own, stood in the bus line, and boarded the bus independently of any help. All this was insisted upon by our teacher for the blind, for, as she explained to us, Mark must remain as independent as he possibly can for as long as he can. This request on her part had to be reinforced many times, for it was only natural for those of us around the school to want to offer help.

For us, Mark's case presented an enormous challenge, which we accepted but have not yet met. The Massachusetts Commission for the Blind flatly turned down all our requests for direct service support for Mark. The commission did this despite the fact that its own regulations call for direct service for blind school-age children, and on the pretext that Public Law 766 is to provide all services for the handicapped between the ages of three and twenty-two. Ironically, even though we took on these financial responsibilities—and they were heavy—the budget for the commission has not been decreased.

Wrestling with Problems

About three years after the launching of our program, we began to detect a certain resentment on the part of the regular classroom teachers and administrators, an annoyance at the amount of publicity we were receiving and the funding advantages we enjoyed. Cases such as the four reviewed above were much discussed because of their complexity, and the media saw them as newsworthy. We were accused of taking funds away from the regular students and spending them on the special-needs students. Actually, by making our regular schools special schools that could offer programs to the handicapped and learning disabled, we were saving untold tax dollars and, more important, helping students to realize their full potential and so develop valuable human resources. The state did not, I think, allow adequate funds or services to flow through to us from the human service agencies. We in education reasoned that as we undertook cases for the human services that had once been under their care, they should relinquish funds from their budget to help support our programs. This remains a bone of contention between education and the human services today. As regards the regular teachers and administrators, their attitude has come full circle; they now realize that having the handicapped in the schools is of benefit to the regular students. Through their involvement with the special-needs teams, the regular staff have learned techniques of behavior

management, assessment skills, and teaching strategies that allow
them to be more effective with regular students as well as meet the
needs of the handicapped and learning disabled. As regards the
state, it set up a system of incentive grants in the late seventies that
rewarded schools financially if they successfully brought children
back from state-run institutions and provided education and support programs for them.[4] The transition of children from the state-
run institutions to the public schools was a relatively smooth process. Problems did arise, however, over private school placement.
An appeals process for parents and schools had been written into
Public Law 766. This process allows parents to disagree with the
education plan that has been drawn up for the special needs of their
child and present their objections to a hearing officer. And it allows
the schools to present their arguments as to why they feel the program they are offering is adequate and appropriate to meet the
child's needs. In our own situation, eight families decided not to
accept the individual education plans presented by our teams. They
placed their children in private schools and sent us the bill for tuition. As the law was then being interpreted by the State Bureau of
Special Education Appeals (a bureau funded by our own State
Department and staffed with lawyers who served as hearing officers), parents were allowed to place their children first, then put
the burden on us to prove that our placement was indeed adequate,
appropriate, and the least restrictive. We had to spend considerable
energy over the first two years of my administration preparing and
defending our position at appeals hearings. It became evident to me
that the first step toward winning an appeals hearing was to meet the
needs of our students whom we sought to bring back from private
school placement. I am sure that every school system in those years
remembers all too vividly the name of the private school that sprung
up in their area advertising widely that their services for the learning
disabled and handicapped were all that could be desired. We prepared our cases, showing why our program could meet the needs of
these privately placed youngsters. These cases were brought
through the appeals process, and our education plans were found to
be adequate and appropriate to meet the students' needs. One by
one, seven of these students returned to our schools, one family
choosing to have their daughter remain in the private placement at

its own expense. This was no mean task. It was very important to succeed in these efforts, for we needed the funds that had been drained out of our budget for private school tuition so that we could apply these moneys to support existing programs and develop further support systems. I give tremendous credit to our attorney, Arthur Murphy, who worked closely with our team and who never once asked anyone to testify about anything he or she did not firmly believe in and feel confident to report on. His chapters on the appeals process (Chapters 6 and 7) are a fascinating story in themselves.

There is a strong case to be made for making regular schools special from a financial point of view, and an examination of the statistics published by Rossmiller, Hale, and Frohreich bear this out.[5] These studies, done from 1970 through 1975, analyze the return on our investment for dollars spent on special education for the handicapped and the learning disabled.

The study shows that taxes were calculated on a salary based on the federal minimum wage ($2.30 at the time of the study) and amounted to $1,121 for one year or $44,840 over forty years, the average work life of a person. By dividing the excess cost for twelve years ($28,536) by the taxes paid in one year ($1,121), a payback period of 25.5 years was determined. When the total excess cost ($28,536) is subtracted from the taxes paid over a forty-year period by a visually handicapped person who had received an education through twelfth grade ($44,840), the result is a long-term saving of $16,304 by the community. If the estimated saving to the community in income-maintenance payments were added to this figure, there would be a total savings of $61,144. Thus, by spending more on a handicapped person's education, the community profits by $61,144 over the span of his or her working life.

In another study, the payback period for a speech-impaired child was 2.3 years with a total long-term saving of $87,076; for a mildly retarded student it was 11.2 years, and when a mildly retarded child was taught academic and work skills instead of being placed in a custodial institution (a not infrequent event), a total long-term saving of $441,289 resulted. The average payback period in this study was found to be 25 years.

This study shows that early opportunities for development lead to success. Similar results have been demonstrated in other studies. Ronald W. Conley, author of *The Economics of Mental Retardation,* reports that the lifetime earnings of mildly retarded adults are six times the cost of their education.[6] He concludes that educational services to the mildly retarded can be justified on the basis of earnings alone. It is, in fact, self-defeating not to provide these services since this would sacrifice a large long-run gain for a small short-run gain.

The success of retarded people in employment depends on their having the opportunity for intellectual and social development in childhood and supportive services as adults. Evidence shows that there are very few intellectually handicapped individuals who do not have potential for gainful employment, and those who cannot actually join the labor force are usually capable of learning self-care skills that can help them to become better integrated into family life.

As I think back over the last decade, I can enthusiastically say that Public Law 766 has proven a boon for the children found to be in need of special care and consideration. It has offered school districts the opportunity to increase staff and build new programs. In returning handicapped and learning-disabled students to our regular schools, not only have we offered superior educational opportunities to them, but they in turn, through their uniqueness, have enriched the general atmosphere of the school—as in the case of Mark, our blind student. Mark's classmates, in reaching out and helping him, are in their turn acquiring a sensitivity and understanding that will stand them in good stead throughout their lives.

No one can accuse us of spending money unwisely, for in fact we are succeeding in great savings in both human resources and tax dollars, as we return children from private and state institutions where per-pupil costs are double and sometimes triple our own.

As I look forward, I can identify some important tasks that must be undertaken. If we are to maintain our existing programs and work toward accepting more handicapped students into our schools, then we must join forces with regular teachers and help them in every way we can to acquire some of the assessment skills, the behavior management skills, and the planning and teaching methods that we have found successful in special education. This means that we must more precisely define that population which will receive special education. Children who are found to have marginal special needs can then have support and encouragement from the regular classroom teacher.

I think we must cut down or even eliminate the waste through duplication of effort that exists within the state's human services. These services must be made to support and complement our special-needs programs in the public schools, and if we continually find unwillingness for this form of cooperation, then I feel strongly that some of the funds allocated to human services should be turned over to the public schools so that we can develop new programs to fill unmet needs.

If we can make progress toward these goals, I see no reason why our objective to serve as many children as have the need in as regular and as normal a setting as possible cannot continue to be considered one of the most important educational objectives for the 1980s.

3
The Team Approach

The Building Planning and Placement Team is the very heart of
our delivery system for special education. These teams must be a
strong and effective extension of the director of special education's
authority in each of the schools in the district. To be effective they
must have clearly defined authority and a well-understood method
of operating that each member subscribes to. Without this base a
team will not be able to stand up to the pressures placed upon it
from school committees, administrators, teachers, parents, and
child advocates.

Defining and Organizing the Team

Each team member should work from the base of an official job
description understood and approved by the school administrators
and the school committee. The job description should contain a
statement covering the desired job qualifications, line of responsibility, job goals, performance responsibilities, terms of employment, and procedures for job performance evaluation.

Every team should have a person designated in a leadership role
and serving as chairperson. The following could serve well as a
model for that person's job description:[1]

Job Description
Building Planning and Placement Team Chairperson
Preamble

The chairperson's job is to facilitate, supervise, and be
responsible for the delivery of services for all special needs

students assigned to a given school building. This includes both students enrolled in the assigned building and students placed in day or residential institutions.

The chairperson is responsible to the director of special education for the overall delivery of services, including the coordination of district policy and procedures aimed at providing a well-organized delivery system for special services. In addition, the chairperson is responsible for cooperating with the building principal to ensure that special-needs policies and procedures are in tune with the philosophy and organization of the individual school.

The chairperson acts as the director of special education's designee in the implementation of Public Law 766 and signs all educational plans emanating from his or her building. Responsibilities in the role are in addition to regular contract positions such as teacher, counselor, or other specialist.

General Definition of Building Planning and Placement Team

The Building Planning and Placement Team is defined as that group of full- and part-time professionals assigned by the director of special education to any given building on a yearly basis. The team diagnoses special needs and delivers such services as psychological counseling, guidance, speech and language therapy, learning disabilities remediation and training, occupational therapy, physical therapy, tutoring, and psychiatric consultation. The team also reviews cases in which a child's grade placement is in question.

Specific Responsibilities of Chairpeople

1. The chairperson screens all referrals, determining the route that referral should take—determining if it falls in the general rubric of Public Law 766, or if services of a diagnostic or remedial nature should be assigned in line with regular building resources.
2. The chairperson, in cooperation with the director of special education and the principal, develops strategies

for handling cases and coordinates efforts of school personnel to develop plans and deliver services.

3. The chairperson presides over core evaluations and coordinates the writing and reviewing of all educational plans.

4. The chairperson is responsible for keeping the records on all cases in order and up to date.

5. The chairperson is responsible for keeping the building principal, the director of special education, and any other involved persons updated on all cases.

6. The chairperson is responsible for providing relevant information to teachers regarding all special-needs students.

7. The chairperson facilitates the transition of special-needs students from one school to another, whether it be within the system or whether it includes out-of-system placement. This may include visiting outside placements, arranging for out-of-system placements to meet a child's needs, and reviewing the progress of children in these placements.

8. The chairperson is responsible for aiding a special-needs student upon graduation or when he or she reaches the 22nd birthday in making a transition from school to other appropriate human services agencies.

9. The chairperson or designee acts as the liaison between the home and the school for special-needs students.

10. The chairperson assists in the development and evaluation of collaborative special needs programs. If a collaborative program is housed in his or her building, a chairperson may have more direct responsibility for coordinating the efforts of program development and evaluation.

11. The chairperson is responsible for facilitating programs with other human service agencies—Department of Mental Health, Welfare, Division of Youth Services, etc.

12. The chairperson is responsible for implementation de-

partment policies as interpreted by the director of special education.

13. The chairperson will assist the director of special education in preparing for the new school year and in closing out the old.

14. The chairperson will be responsible for duties outlined in this document and any other duties assigned by the director of special education.

Evaluation

1. The chairperson will be appointed upon the recommendation of the superintendent of schools after a review of evaluation with the director of special education, on a yearly basis. Performance in the role will be evaluated by the director, after consultation with the building principal.

2. Regular contract roles such as teacher, counselor, or other specialist will be evaluated separately from the chairperson's role.

It is absolutely essential to the team's success that it collect all the data it needs from parents, specialists' reports, clinics, and hospital reports and observations before it makes its final recommendation. The team must appreciate that the parents of special-needs children have frequently been through a great deal of stress and probably have received some unacceptable and confusing messages from professionals before reaching the Building Planning and Placement Team for help. It is therefore important that the members present themselves as a team that is totally united in its message and, to a member, support its recommendation. Anything short of this will add to the parents' anxiety.

Any team that wishes to grow as a professional unit should become proficient in the arts of group dynamics. One way to ensure that growth takes place is to set aside regular times for conducting self-evaluations of the team's performance. It should be the chairperson's responsibility to set out a model the team will accept for the evaluation of its performance. Team members should be reminded at the outset that their job is a high-risk undertaking and assured that the process of collective decision-making will increase the likelihood of making sound decisions. Mistakes will be made, however, and evaluation will not be based on a failure/success basis. One workable model that can be employed is for the chairperson to assign alternating team members the responsibility of recording and analyzing team sessions. At certain times videotaping is a useful method for recording sessions. Even if parents are present, they often don't object if the purpose of the camera is explained. The real advantage of taping a session is that it allows the entire team to do its analysis of the session, whereas if a member does the recording in writing, the impressions put forward are of course biased. In either case it is wise to agree beforehand what the team holds as standards of operation. Some of these standards would logically be such things as sticking to the task, listening while others put forward their points, noting whether members were ready and on time with their reports, noting whether members conveyed a sense of caring about parents' points of view, admitting errors, checking whether all resources were tapped, reviewing whether objectives for meeting were made clear at the outset, noting whether parents were informed of their rights under the law and, very important, whether the meeting concluded with a clear sense of what was to happen next. These points could well represent the major focus for team discussion, and it is important that the members determine some of the areas where they wish to make professional growth and then proceed to set reasonable goals to achieve these ends.

It has been made clear that a written agreement as to the line authority given a team is of paramount importance. Our department conducted a survey in 1977 in which the administrators of special education of twenty-three surrounding towns and cities were asked ten questions about the scope of their responsibilities. The final question was: "As administrators of special education, do you see it as important that you have a clearly defined line of authority from the superintendent of schools to yourself and from yourself to your department staff?" Eighteen towns and cities completed the questionnaire, and all eighteen answered yes to the above question. What is particularly interesting is that although many towns and cities saw the importance of having line authority equal to or above that of a school principal, many did not have such an arrangement that had been clearly defined and approved by the school committees. Even more revealing is the fact that the high attrition rate in that state found among the directors of special education falls largely among that group which tries to administer programs without a direct line of authority to do so.

The Role and Responsibilities of the Team

Once a team's organizational structure is well defined, the team should be urged to function as an integral part of the school. The nature of its role gives it certain rights and responsibilities that it must, by law, carry out. It must give prompt attention to referrals, conduct assessments, and deal with delicate negotiations around getting individual educational plans accepted.

The team must not let this demanding work prevent its members from showing an interest in and supporting the school as a whole. There is a certain subtlety here in that the team has power and authority outside the sphere of the building principal. It must not flaunt this power, for the team needs the building administrator's support just as the building principal needs the team's support, and so the subtle balance is struck.

The establishment of the team as the operating mode described here best allows for service delivery of the handicapped within the philosophical framework of the new roles and functions for special education. In contrast to the view held in the 1960s—that one labeled children so that they could be grouped together homogeneously and segregated from the mainstream of regular education—we now view a child with a disability not as a different kind of a child, but rather as an ordinary child with a special need. This philosophical position, once taken, credits the school as being the preferred setting socially for educating all children.

A team, having carried out its assessment plan, sets about the job of constructing an individual education plan. The members describe the student's present circumstances and levels of functioning. They outline the measures to be taken to achieve defined objectives, and they state the services and conditions under which these are to be carried out. There is that part of the individual plan which in the education and care of children is above and beyond, supplementary to, or different from the education offered by teachers of regular students. The individual plan may specify special methods or arrangements for low-incident cases of the severely handicapped or hearing-impaired student who requires a modified curriculum, special equipment to be used by the regular teacher, or certain desirable social arrangements that will prove best in nurturing positive behavior. All these arrangements that directly involve regular teachers must be carefully negotiated by the team.

Program Options

The team members have direct control over several program options. The number of options depends largely on the financial resources at the team's disposal. If special-education administrators allow funds to be drained from their budgets by unnecessary private placements for children, they will not have the funds to develop their own programs in the least restrictive environment and will find themselves in serious financial and eventually political difficulty. Programs developed internally to meet the needs of handicapped children have the advantage of strict quality controls and dramatic savings on transportation costs, and, what is very important, they will be credited with having upheld the letter and spirit of the law. The options include separate residential day facilities that provide for all needs outside the regular school, full-time special classes in the regular schools, part-time classes in the regular schools, or ordinary classes with support services to the regular teachers.

In the following paragraphs I describe the options available to teams in our own school system. You will see that they are very different from those options available to the learning disabled and handicapped in the previous decade of public education.

Residential placement with a built-in educational component was used only once by a team at the elementary-school level. In this particular case, we sought outside placement only after trying to provide a substantially separate program in an ordinary school and discovering that we were not meeting our goals either at school or at home. It took six months for us to locate an appropriate facility and to work out a cost-sharing agreement with the Department of Mental Health. Such provisions are not called for with any frequency; however, it is necessary that a team have residential placement as an option. Indeed, if the public schools were to become more frequently involved in finding such placements and in monitoring children's progress, a more efficient and equitable system of cost sharing would have to be worked out.

Full-time special classes in the regular schools are distributed fairly evenly among the buildings to allow for an optimal advantage for integrating regular and special students. Obviously, if one were to select one school and establish half a dozen special classes in it, one would be creating an atmosphere of more "specialness." At our high school we had a prevocational/occupational education program for cognitively delayed adolescents. The program prepared children for functioning in the working world through study in a self-contained classroom and carefully monitored work experiences. Through small groups and one-on-one tutoring, the educational component of this program developed skills in communication, daily living, and socialization. The work component for the program progressed from closely supervised in-school work experiences to more independent out-of-school placements. All the students in this program had the option of attending a social club at the school.

The department also supported a self-contained classroom program for students who were not successful in the regular program. We chose to call it our Structured Learning Program. The Building Planning and Placement Team considered students for the program who it felt had potential for growth in social and behavioral skills. The program design called for a self-contained setting in the regular high school. The intent was to provide a safe, controlled environment for intervention.

Each of our new programs was carefully researched and usually written up by a team over the summer for implementation in the fall. To illustrate this process, let's look at the project design of the Structured Learning Program, a high-school-based program.

The Structural Learning Program: A Design for the High School[2]

The composition of the Structural Learning Program for grades 9, 10, 11, and 12 is outlined by the team as follows:

- A fourteen-year-old high school student had broken the behavioral contract made with school staff. In dealing with the inevitable confrontation, the student first denied the misbehavior, then ardently suggested that the staff member observing the infraction "didn't have to tell," and finally explained that unacceptable behavior had occurred because of poor vision and eyes that "fluttered uncontrollably."

- A fifteen-year-old high school student, unable to deal with two friends at once, fabricated a story to break up his initial friendship. When confronted with the results of his lie and the trouble that it had caused, he was unable to assume responsibility for the trouble, nor did he show real remorse.

- A sixteen-year-old student refused to participate in group activities or to obey school rules. She constantly demanded that school staff get her a job at a high salary but was unable to seek a job herself or to accept the job at minimum wage obtained for her. When she did finally accept a job, she covered her errors in handling money by "borrowing" from other employees' funds and was fired. It was "not her fault."

Observation of such students in a high school setting would indicate that although we are making progress dealing with young people who do not function well academically, we are not making the same progress with young people who do not function well socially.

There have been obstacles to progress in working with adolescents on social skills. We have made great efforts to mainstream handicapped youngsters, equipping them with academic support systems but not with social support systems other than counselor availability in times of crisis. Our high schools do not allow us the same flexibility for meeting social needs as they do for meeting academic needs. We have resource rooms with specialists and tutors to provide academic remediation or academic support. Socially we encourage students to join school activities by making suggestions or by reminding students of meetings, but we find that this is insufficient. At times we solve problems by getting students out of the building on work-study programs or by taking away all of a student's free time. We have often used the same intervention strategies and discipline strategies for adolescents that function at very different levels. We employ reasoning strategies at levels too far removed from the student's level of functioning, or we suspend students from school for a day or so to "cool off." Neither strategy changes the behavior of some of our students.

Defining Problems in Social Development

At first glance, students who function poorly in high schools seem to behave as if they were experiencing emotional problems, as if they were less capable intellectually, or as if they were much younger than their years. The issue of poor social functioning appears to be complex, and we may indeed be dealing with several different types of problems.

Three different types of social difficulties stand out. The first is the problem of the cognitively limited adolescent. Although this student may well have stronger skills in some areas than others, the student has cognitive as well as social delay. Intellectually and socially, this student functions like a younger person.

A second problem is the student with a nonverbal learning disability in social perception. This entails an inability to identify and recognize the meaning and significance of the behavior of others. According to Johnson and Myklebust,[3] this student is unable to perceive and interpret nonverbal behaviors, has a confused perceptual field resulting in inaccurate estimations of space, has difficulties learning about territorial boundaries, is naive in social interactions with the opposite sex, has poor affective sensitivity, lacks the verbal fluency required to produce divergent responses in conversational language, and has poor elaboration and difficulty shifting in interpretational approaches (such as when talking to adults versus peers).

A third group of adolescents with social problems are the young people exhibiting a dyplasia.[4] The term refers to a split in developmental levels whereby the affective and cognitive levels have not progressed at equal rates, resulting in malfunctioning. One example of this type of problem may be the student with immature character development. This student moves toward adulthood unable to defer immediate gratification, enter into give-and-take relationships with others, or recognize that he or she is only one

part of a class and not the center of the universe. Most important
of all, the student is unaware of being responsible for his or her
own behavior. Thus, he or she is unable to receive negative data
and self-correct. The student with immature character development tends to assume that special consideration is his or her natural right. The student avoids effort unless it is fun, is unable to
finish a task that involves overcoming obstacles, and constantly
tests limits.

There are other subgroups of young people within the population of adolescents who do not function well socially. These include students with a variety of emotional problems that are
chronic or adolescent adjustment reactions.

The theoretical base for looking at problems in social development has been clinical or cognitive, and only recently have more
useful theories been formulated upon which to base interventions.
There are now a variety of developmental-stage theories that are
useful in understanding the high school student who does not function well. The stages are variously labeled by the theorists, and
each new writer relabels the stages depending on which aspect of
growth he or she wishes to focus on. It is to be remembered that
stages are only a way of marking developments in a process of
growth. The descriptions of functioning at various levels given
below are very broad, since I have attempted to integrate various
theorists' interpretations of behaviors.

In characterizing high school students' level of functioning, we
should keep in mind that a student may function well even at a
lower or delayed level of functioning, and the student of concern is
the one who is functioning poorly at his or her level of functioning,
whatever that level may be.

The first level of functioning has various labels. This level of
functioning is sometimes seen among the developmentally delayed
students found in high schools. A student at this level seems to
reason logically but is reasoning on the basis of what that person
perceives as real. The world is seen from an egocentric point of
view, that is, with the student at the center. There is avoidance of
punishment, and the consequences of an action determine its good-
ness or badness.[5] This student is dependent and sees other people in
terms of what they can give to his or her needs. The high school

student in this stage is seen as "incorrigible."[6] This stage is a one-way prospect in dealing with others. The student can differentiate between his or her own perspective and that of others, but there is no give-and-take here. A good friend does what one wants him to do. In a group, one "copies" or "shows" others. Individuals "bunch" together to do a concrete activity. This student is said to lack impulse control The student is preoccupied with impulses because they are so difficult to control and can lead to punishment, which is seen as retaliatory. In a way, "rather than having impulses . . . , the child *is* his or her impulses and perceptions."[7] This student is vulnerable and somewhat confused, and waits to be given in to.

A second type of student can think logically about the here-and-now world and about things that would previously have been worked out in a trial-and-error action. This student can learn and follow rules and can form assumptive hypotheses about how the world works. The assumptive hypothesis allows students to alter the facts to fit their hypotheses rather than alter the hypotheses themselves.[8] It also allows students to ignore all cues that their *modus operandi* may be incorrect. It allows them to give up or be irresponsible when required to engage in something they don't want to do, or when they can't solve a problem because they did not follow directions that were contrary to their original hypothesis.

This student tries to please and gain approval; yet what is right is what the student needs and occasionally what others need. Reciprocity, fairness, and equal sharing are interpreted in terms of "You scratch my back, I'll scratch yours." The consequences of an act are differentiated from human need.[9] The student is opportunistic and hedonistic. The rules are used to gain his or her own ends, which are often to avoid work, look for fun, and get nice things. A person at this level gets away with whatever he can, by deception or pretense if necessary, as rules are seen as a loss of freedom.[10] This student can be shamed but does not show real remorse, nor does he or she assume real responsibility. Short-term reward and punishment are anticipated, but controls are fragile. Circumstances or other people are blamed for problems. Others are viewed in terms of what can be "gotten" from them. In interpersonal relationships, this student is preoccupied with gaining

advantage, gaining reward, and avoiding punishment. Conceptions of friendship include a concern for what each person thinks
of the other, and conformity is motivated to avoid embarrassment.
Relationships hold together because of similar likes in specific
social activities and because of the mechanism of exchange of
favors. Groups are seen as chains of twosomes, but the basic purpose of friendship is to serve separate self-interests rather than
mutual interests.

Such students are rewarded by being told that they are correct,
and, given this feedback, they can then praise themselves. The
student has a private world and so has organized internal experience as well as the outside world. This student can effect
"what happens." If this student misbehaves, his or her concern is
the consequences of others' finding out. Since the student cannot
integrate his own needs-perspective with someone else's, he or she
has "to await or anticipate the actual movements or reactions of
others to keep [his or her] world coherent." High school students
in this stage are manipulators or operators because they *have* to
be, in order to regulate their relations to the environment.[11] It is
the student at this level in whom we are primarily interested.

A next higher level or more integrated student can take into
consideration the thoughts of other people and can deal with ab-
stract verbal problems. This student is self-reflective and can talk
about inner feelings and motivations. At first this ability is generalized, and the student either has difficulty distinguishing his own
thought from what others are thinking or believes that others are
as preoccupied with him as he is himself. Students perform for this
imaginary audience and assume that everyone else shares whatever self-evaluation they make about themselves. Because adolescents can conceptualize exceptions to rules, they also at first think
that they are exempt from rules that hold for others.[12]

At this level, students conform to personal expectations and social order. They conform to images of what is majority behavior and
judge behavior by intention. Good behavior is at first what pleases
others; later, there is an orientation toward authority, rules, and
duty.[13] At first, the group is the family and the student is concerned
with appearance, social acceptance, and reputation. Disapproval is
most feared. Later, there is an increase in self-awareness, but ex-

ceptions to rules are still somewhat stereotyped. Here relationships are ongoing and seen as a sharing of mutual interests. The relationships are exclusive and possessive at first.[14] The group is seen as a community bound by common interests. Conformity is maintained by a threat of social ostracism—the fear of being different from the group's norms or of being left out. The concern for uniformity is too great.[15] A student at this level is not typically seen as having a major problem at the high school level, and although a student may function poorly at this level, the major focus of this program is the student at the less integrated or developmentally advanced levels.

The student on whom we will focus is a student who is variously labeled concrete operational, imperial, self-protective, opportunistic, delta, stage 2, stage 3, instrumental, hedonistic, safety-oriented, power-oriented or manipulator, depending on which theorist you are reading. This student is often receiving special services and may be referred for behavioral or emotional reasons or for peer difficulties. Interpersonal functioning is a primary concern, and these students draw attention because they do not recognize their responsibility for their actions at preconformist stages of ego development.

Intervention Strategies

When we turn to intervention strategies, it is helpful to look at recent contributions to theory that are useful in the development of programming. Loevinger pointed out that ego level and social responsiveness are limited by intellectual level.[16] In addition, researchers have found that there can be a discrepancy between a child's social understanding as measured by current techniques (discussion-type responses to hypothetical interpersonal dilemma) and a child's actual behavior in a social situation.[17] Kegan points out that development can be extremely painful, accompanied by a staggering sense of loss for some students.[18]

Where a person is in the developmental framework may be far more crucial to his or her employability than any set of trade-related skills. Forms of treatment that presume capacities that students don't have, such as the ability to be a member of an interpersonal community, will not work. Lastly, poor functioning should not be automatically labeled psychopathology.

Real growth takes time and stimulation. Change is unlikely unless the environment and expectations facilitate it. When faced with situations or observations that are incompatible with the student's mode of perceiving his or her environment, the student can ignore parts of the situation that did not fit or can distort them to fit his level of functioning.

Piaget believed that social pressures drive a person to grow.[19] Erikson believed that a student becomes internally differentiated as a means of mastering loss or frustration in his relations with other people.[20] Kohlberg has found that higher-level functioning models help move a student forward.[21] Dember proposed that a person tends to sample stimuli just a little more complex than the level at which he or she usually functions.[22] These stimuli are considered to be "pacers." Parents or teachers can serve as pacers, for example. Loevinger points out that pacers at a slightly advanced level can provide stimulus for growth without danger of losing ground themselves in groups of persons of similar ego level.[23] New stimuli are reacted to negatively at first.

The various theories guard against the assumption that changes can be effected in a classroom experience of brief duration, such as several weeks. However, many studies have been designed for one class period daily of curriculum and have effected some small change. The total surrounding environment must support the change, however, and some experiments in creating a "community" experience conflict with higher authorities or the wider community.

What is needed is a pacer model with firm, reasonable expectations to foster growth. In addition, a safe, controlled environment that will support growth is necessary, and enough time is needed to effect the change. Even at that, change will be small; a half step is maximal expectation. One goal of intervention, then, may involve a half-stage change to a more complex level of development. This would make sense when a child's cognitive understandings and actual behavior match, yet the individual is not functioning well enough for successful employment or is developmentally behind his or her peers. Another goal, however, might involve bringing actual behavior into line with cognitive understandings. Still another goal is to enable students to function successfully at the stage they are in at the time. A student may be well adjusted and function effectively at any stage of ego development. A last point to be made regarding intervention is that the type of intervention must be aimed at the stage of development in which the individual is currently functioning. The student that we are interested in here needs help gaining rewards without simultaneously provoking punishment or retaliation, as observed by Swenson.[24] Behavioral management with a cognitive orientation is appropriate. Swensen also suggests reality therapy.

Program Design

A self-contained classroom will provide the necessary safe, controlled environment for intervention. These students need remedial efforts that involve training procedures. These procedures will be less obvious in a self-contained classroom. The general strategy is to create *personal* goals with a system of behavioral analysis and management using contingency intervention and then work toward *interpersonal* goals in a step-by-step procedure.

Academic goals will be individually set from achievement test performance in both language arts and mathematics. Writing and spelling goals will be set on the basis of writing samples. One of the language arts blocks will consist of language development under the direction of the language pathologist. The social studies model is based on a pilot program entitled "Current Events and Political Awareness" that was run during 1979–80. Academic work in this area will comprise five blocks of the day.

Following Piaget's belief that organization is basic to concept development, the teaching approach will begin by focusing on organizing information for students. Students will then learn conceptual self-organization and instruction. Goals include teaching students problem definition, problem approach, focus of attention, self-reinforcement, and self-evaluation. This approach is called cognitive behavior modification.[25] The procedure will be utilized in both the academic and social training aspects of the program.

In addition, there will be three blocks of counseling per week, which is a special case of social learning and will provide training in social perception and affective sensitivity, a deliberate psychological educational training program also run as a pilot during the 1979–

80 school year. In addition to materials already developed, both simulations and human relations training materials will be incorporated, as well as film strips of social dilemmas.[26] Open blocks will consist of activities designed to build cooperative skills involving art, making marionettes for play production, sharing, and group planning. "Adventure Counseling" will be offered in the second semester.[27] Students will participate in at least one mainstream class if they can handle it. They will set goals, evaluate their progress toward goals, and reward themselves weekly.

The course units will consist of the following:

1. Structured English
2. Basic Functional Math
3. Human Relations
4. Attitudes, Skills, and Careers
5. People, the Press, and Politics
6. Communications

The project objectives are as follows:

1. Given that specific academic deficits are ascertained through achievement testing, individual academic goals will be set and reached through a series of tasks designed to meet each goal in basic skill areas.
2. Given that organization is basic to the enhancement of cognitive and social skills, students will internalize organizational strategies through self-instructional training.
3. With the help of behavioral management, students will learn the techniques of problem-solving, goal-setting, self-evaluation, and self-reinforcement.
4. Through various group training experiences, students will advance their social perception and skills of social interaction.
5. Students will increase understanding of social interactions through writing plays and presenting them with marionettes they have constructed themselves.

Program evaluation will consist of preprogram and postprogram achievement tests and writing sample. Preprogram and postprogram psychological testing will consist of the House–Tree–Person Test, Jr.–Sr. Personality Questionnaire, Tennessee Self-Concept

Scale, and Bristol Social Adjustment Guides. Piagetian evaluation, where applicable, and Structure of the Intellect Learning Abilities measures will be utilized.[28]

Expected outcomes are as follows: students will demonstrate increased academic skill on achievement tests; increased organizational skills by improved day-to-day performance as reflected in subjective teacher evaluation and by report of observations by the project director; the ability to set goals and to evaluate progress toward meeting those goals as reflected by their notebooks; and an enhanced ability to interact in groups by various testing procedures and by successful interactions in the mainstream.

The Structural Learning Program design was carefully planned during the summer vacation. Those involved were paid a stipend over and above salary for their efforts. The proposal was reviewed by me and implemented by the school psychologist, who also served as Building Planning and Placement Team chairperson. The program achieved a high rate of success; students responded to the goal-setting process and self-evaluation far beyond our expectations. Such use of summertime for planning should be encouraged, for it is an effective way to utilize talent.

Program Options at the Middle-School Level

At the middle-school level (grades 6, 7, and 8) our teams may consider placing cognitively delayed students in a program designed for younger children. The program strives to help each student to achieve his or her highest level of functioning academically, vocationally, and socially. The students are integrated with regular students only for art, music, gym, lunch, and recess. Domestic arts and workshop programs are designed to provide life skills and prevocational training.

At the same location the teams may consider the Developmental Language Program a self-contained program designed to meet the needs of middle-school-age children who demonstrate moderate to severe speech and language disorders with accompanying learning difficulties. This program is designed as a part of a local educational collaborative since a small school system does not always turn up enough students for a program and recruitment from other locations becomes necessary. It can be to the advantage of a school district to take the initiative by running programs for its own children. This means that children can stay in their own town and, not least important, economy in transportation can be realized.

The speech and language disorders exhibited by these children may include (1) receptive language disorders in the areas of comprehension of vocabulary, ability to follow directions, comprehension of statements and questions (receptive aphasia); (2) expressive language disorders in the areas of vocabulary usage, word retrieval, ability to formulate sentences (expressive aphasia); (3) articulation disorders in the areas of delayed articulation, apraxia, and/or dysarthria. These children additionally demonstrate various learning difficulties in the areas of visual–auditory perception and memory, reading and/or reading readiness, math and fine/gross motor skills.

In order to create an environment where the Developmental Language Program students can interact with other students of different ages and abilities, the staff seeks, whenever possible, to integrate each child's learning experience with the mainstream of the regular classrooms. Integration may include both academic and social interactions with the children's peers.

Based on each child's strengths and weaknesses, an appropriate program is designed and implemented to meet the child's needs in all speech, language, and learning areas. The Developmental Language Program follows the regular school curriculum. Academic instruction includes math, reading, social studies, science, language, fine motor skills, and visual–auditory skills. These areas are covered in individual and group sessions. Social and emotional development is promoted throughout the school day. Children receive art, music, and physical education instruction from the specialists in the school. Additionally, each student receives individual and small-group speech and language therapy, occupational therapy, and counseling as needed. Parent involvement is encouraged and is an important aspect of the program. This is accomplished through various means, such as daily communication books, progress conferences, written progress reports, and parent observations of classroom activities. Through the joint efforts of parents and teachers, the children's needs become more clearly defined and therefore more successfully met. This particular program was designed by me with the assistance with the speech and language specialists. The daily responsibility, as it was a collaborative program, was assumed by the chairperson of the Building Planning and Placement Team.

Early Childhood Program

The last option the teams have in this category is a self-contained Early Childhood Program at an elementary school. For this program the children are selected by a rather elaborate screening procedure conducted in the late summer before school starts. These three- and four-year-olds fall in the category of mild to severely handicapped children.

The Early Childhood Program is designed to meet the individual special needs of children before they enter kindergarten. A screening evaluation is conducted to determine if there are any physical, social–emotional, speech/language, hearing, or visual handicaps that indicate a need for early intervention.

Classes are taught by an early-childhood education specialist and meet four or five times per week for a morning or afternoon session. Specialist consultations and services for speech/language pathology, audiology, physical therapy, occupational therapy, learning disabilities, and child psychology are available as needed.

The program is based on the belief that young children learn in a developmental sequence through interaction with people and materials. Language is seen to develop interdependently with social, emotional, and cognitive skills. The curriculum includes many activities that will provide maximum opportunities to learn language and to meet individual speech and language goals.

Music, movement education, language arts, science, math, art activities, puzzles, sand-and-water play, and symbolic play activities are part of the daily curriculum. Teachers involve children in symbolic play activities to help them to learn about the meaning of words, the sequence of events, and cause-and-effect relationships. Symbolic play and natural interactions, such as snacktime, are also used to model developmentally appropriate language structures for each child.

Parent involvement is seen as an integral and vital part of this program. Parents have the opportunity to observe children in work and play activities from a location separated from the classroom by a one-way window. In addition, parents are encouraged to meet regularly in a small group with an early-childhood specialist or a speech/language pathologist to share ideas and feelings and to discuss language stimulation techniques and issues of child development. Parents also involve themselves in the classroom with specific tasks with individual children.

The programs described thus far are the options the teams have at their disposal for the placement of students within our school district. Additional options were available to the teams for placement of students in other districts where collaborative programs were available and appropriately met the teams' needs.

Learning Centers

The next set of options for the team consists of part-time special classes located in regular schools. These programs we refer to as our learning centers. They are designed for students who have a variety of handicaps and learning disabilities. Students may attend the centers for as little as one period or for a full morning or afternoon. Each student has an individualized education plan that takes into account learning style, levels of social and emotional growth, academic levels and needs. The centers have all the latest audiovisual equipment and very recently have been equipped with computers and attendant software.

Support programs for hearing-impaired students are available throughout all grades. The goal for these students is almost total integration into regular classes, with a period or two set aside for a support person such as a teacher of the hearing impaired to help students individually with homework assignments and to discuss any unresolved issues that may arise. A support teacher for the hearing impaired is responsible for training regular teachers in the use of transmitter and phonic ear equipment. Support programs are in place for the physically handicapped population. Each student must be considered on an individual basis after the team consults with our occupational therapist. Again the goal is for maximum integration into regular classes with support as needed. Behavioral disorders are dealt with in a variety of settings within the schools. Throughout the schools one finds counseling groups, play therapy groups, and Adventure Counseling activity groups.

The team may consider students for part-time placement or classroom support by a speech and language pathologist. We provide a complete range of speech, language, and communication services. In our setting we have addressed handicaps in auditory and listening skills, hearing impairment, apraxia, stuttering, facial anomalies, cleft palate, and severe physical handicaps resulting from cerebral palsy. The various communication systems for the nonverbal child are beginning to expand in number and sophistication because of breakthroughs in computer technology. It is a fact today that a physically handicapped student who does not have the use of hands or feet can employ a computer keyboard to which he or she may give voice signals that are picked up by the computer terminal.

You can now see how comprehensive a school system's programs must be in order that the handicapped and learning-disabled population's needs can be met in the public schools. Some programs start out in the regular schools in a very separate way. However, the education plans for these children contain the seeds for future integration. Some children can be integrated in the regular classrooms right away, while others will have to spend most of their time in programs separate from the mainstream students. We see these students benefiting tremendously by being a part of a regular school's recreation, lunch programs, and cultural assemblies and enjoying the distinctive advantage of having friends in school who are neighbors at home.

The spirit of the public law is certainly to make regular schools special. How incongruous it seems, that during the first eight years of the law the Bureau of Special Appeals has ruled on over half of its cases that schools are *not* to have the opportunity to provide special programs in regular schools, but must pay for private programs. This seems to run counter to all that we are trying to do. Chapter 6, on the appeals process, in part explains why this has

4
The Massachusetts Human Service Systems

The agony, frustration, and sheer physical exhaustion that plague the professional life of human service workers is probably equal to those of the clients they serve. These professionals—speech pathologists, psychiatric social workers, nurses, doctors, occupational therapists, and many others—are trained to serve a residential as well as a community-based client population that ranges from the elderly to adolescent drug addicts. Their frustration stems from poor management systems, ill-defined populations, and sometimes, although not always, inadequate budgets.

The fact that the populations of the human services and of special education overlap and that many of the same kinds of professionals work in both fields would seem to dictate a need to enact laws to ensure that cooperation, joint planning, and case sharing are carried out with a maximum of efficiency. Unfortunately, such laws do not exist and confusion reigns.

History of Human Service Systems in Massachusetts

It will be useful to step back a moment and review the origins of the human services. The Executive Office of Human Services (EOHS) found its way into Bay State law through the Acts and Resolves of the Great and General Court, passed in 1969, which are described as follows.

Section 16. The following state agencies are hereby declared to be within the executive office of human services: the department of public health and all other state agencies within said department, including the commission on hypertension, the drug addiction rehabilitation board, the board of review established by section five E of chapter one hundred and eleven, and the several advisory councils established by sections two B, four D, four F and fifty-five of said chapter; the department of public welfare and all other state agencies within said department; the department of mental health, including the several advisory councils established by sections eleven, twelve and sixteen of chapter nineteen, the several institutions within said department and their boards of trustees, and all other state agencies within said department; the department of correction, including the parole board and all other state agencies within said department; the advisory council on home and family; the commissioner of veterans' services; the boards of trustees of the Soldiers' Home in Massachusetts and the board of trustees of the Soldiers' Home in Holyoke; the youth service board; the advisory committee on service to youth; the division of youth service, including the several institutions within said division; The Massachusetts rehabilitation commission and the advisory council; the boxers' fund board; the health and welfare commission; and the Massachusetts commission for the blind and its advisory board, and all other state agencies within said commission.

Nothing in this section shall be construed as conferring any powers or imposing any duties upon the secretary with respect to the foregoing agencies except as expressly provided by law.[1]

Nine years later, in 1978, the EOHS laws were amended as follows, providing for the Office of Children, statewide advisory councils, and a Department of Social Services. The amended material is indicated by italics.

The following state agencies are hereby declared to be within the executive office of human services: *the office for children, including the councils for children and the statewide advisory council established by sections seven and eight of chapter twenty-eight A, the department of social services, in-cluding the area advisory boards and statewide advisory council established by sections thirteen and sixteen of chapter eighteen B, the department of public health and all other agencies within said department, including the commission on hypertension, the drug addiction rehabilitation board, and the several advisory councils established by sections four D,*[2] *four F and fifty-five of chapter one hundred and eleven, but excluding such divisions and personnel which relate to the areas of environmental health, including air pollution con-trol, noise regulation, community sanitation, water supply and water quality, noisome trades and sanitary landfills; the department of public welfare and all* other state agencies within said department; *the commission on supplemental se-curity income,* the department of mental health, including the several advisory councils established by sections eleven, twelve and sixteen of chapter nineteen, the several in-stitutions within said department and their boards of trust-ees and all other state agencies within said department; the department of corrections, including the parole board and all other state agencies within said department; the advisory council on home and family, the commissioner of veterans' services; the board of trustees of the Soldiers' Home in Massachusetts and the board of trustees of the Soldiers' Home in Holyoke; the youth service board,[3] the advisory committee on service to youth; the division of youth ser-vice, including the several institutions within said division; the Massachusetts rehabilitation commission and the ad-visory council; the boxers' fund board; the health and wel-fare commission; the nutrition board; the health facilities appeals board; the rate setting commission established by section thirty-two and the Massachusetts commission for the blind and its advisory board, and all other state agencies within said commission.

Nothing in this section shall be construed as conferring any powers or imposing any duties upon the secretary with respect to the foregoing agencies except as expressly pro-vided by law; *provided, however, that the secretary shall*

*establish uniform regional and area boundaries for all
agencies within the executive office of human services and
further provided that the secretary shall establish uniform
intake and referral forms, uniform contracting and payment
procedures, and uniform standards for the monitoring and
evaluation of all human services programs.*

Amended by St. 1978, c. 552/4.[4]

1978 Amendment. St. 1978, c. 552/4, an emergency act, approved July 22, 1978, and by section 47 made effective upon its passage, inserted "including the councils for children and the statewide advisory council established by sections seven and eight of chapter twenty-eight A, the department of social services, including the area advisory boards and the statewide advisory council established by sections thirteen and sixteen of chapter eighteen B," near the beginning of the first paragraph; and added the proviso in the second paragraph.

St. 1978, c. 552, amended this section in conformity with establishment by the act of the department of social services within the executive office of human services. See G.L. c. 18B/1, and the note thereunder.

1979 Amendment. St. 1979, c. 677/4, approved Nov. 3, 1979, and for which an emergency declaration by the Governor was filed November 7, 1979, was repealed by the voters on November 4, 1980. As added by St. 1979, c. 677, the third paragraph read:

The secretary of human services may, notwithstanding the provisions of section forty-five of chapter thirty or chapter thirty-one, but subject to the approval of the governor and to appropriation, appoint such senior staff, including undersecretaries, deputy secretaries, assistant secretaries, a general counsel, a budget director and executive assistants, as the secretary determines to be appropriate; provided, however, that such appointments shall number no more than nine. Each person appointed to such senior staff position shall have experience and skill in the field of functions of such position; shall receive such salary as the secretary shall determine, subject to the approval of the governor; and, shall devote full time to the duties of the office.

Code of Massachusetts Regulations

Human services agency, executive office, included in agencies, see 101 CMR 8.01.
Cross References
Rehabilitation commission, establishment of regional offices, see c. -/75.

Special Education versus the Human Services

Over sixteen years ago laws were passed in Massachusetts that called for a comprehensive system of human service delivery. Just over thirteen years ago Public Law 766 was passed calling for a comprehensive delivery of service to handicapped and learning-disabled students ages three through twenty-one. In the case of the human services, clients were categorized according to their needs, while the special-education students were stripped of their labels and all children identified were to receive services from funds raised by the cities and towns. Neither situation is highly desirable. The human services—made up of the Departments of Public Welfare, Youth Service, Rehabilitation, Mental Health, Public Health, Social Services, the Commission for the Blind, and the Office for Children—often ran short of funds when legislatures decided to make cuts in budgets, while special educators, under Public Law 766, found it hard to reach a consensus as to whom it was to serve. The human services tended to take the position, as did advocacy groups of parents, that 766 should pay the bills unless they could prove they were not responsible. Long-drawn-out and expensive appeals cases, paid for by the cities and towns, grew out of this unfortunate tangle of bureaucratic machinery.

These circumstances set the scene for an exhausting and unnecessary struggle between education and the human services. In case after case, the Department of Mental Health attempted to shift its responsibilities on education by refusing to pay for or even cost-share cases that rightfully were its own. The department succeeded in maneuvering these case costs into the domain of the public schools. The Commission for the Blind stopped giving direct service to blind children between the ages of three and twenty-two. The commission sent out missives telling the special educators that it would be more than willing to send along a consultant to the schools to tell them what they needed to do, but never offered any direct service.

In our own school system we logged fifteen phone calls on different days to the Commission for the Blind, placed person-to-person calls to the director of that office, and were given different excuses each time why the director could not talk with us. We followed these phone calls with letters detailing the kind of help we needed for a student who was rapidly going blind.

As it turned out, the student of our concern is now totally blind, and we have willingly provided and paid for her mobility training, a stair glide, and trained staff that have met her needs over the past eight years. It is not that we did this work grudgingly, only that the Commission for the Blind has been allowed to take all direct service for blind children out of the schools and keep and/or increase its own budget levels, while we in special education have had to learn about the education of the blind in the mainstream of public education without being given funds to pay for the job. These inefficiencies and duplications of effort are what must be corrected.

The Department of Public Health pursued the public school special educators to provide funds to pay for children placed in nursing homes. In one documented case, a nursing home caring for a child in a coma wrote up a pamphlet that described the educational services this type of child should receive and billed the public schools.

In October of 1978, the Division of Special Education circulated a document called "A Guide to Human Services for School Managers"; actually it was a guide for administrators of special education, and the introduction had the effrontery to say that since the implementation of Chapter 766, one of the major issues has been the need for improved coordination and cooperation between the agencies within the human services system and the local schools— and that one impediment to this coordination was the lack of understanding of human services by school managers. This statement really rubbed salt into the wounds inflicted by the human services on special education. Special-education directors understood only too well what human services were mandated to do.

The human services had been responsible for serving many of the students that public education now was called upon to serve, children who were blind, crippled, not toilet-trained, deaf, emotionally disturbed, apraxic, aphasic, et cetera, et cetera. Human service budgets stayed the same, and some even went up, but very little direct help to the schools became available.

A Guide to the Human Services

The following guide to the human services (issued by its Executive Office) is used here as a ready reference to summarize the purposes of the various agencies within the human services.

Department of Public Welfare

The Department of Public Welfare (DPW) has three administrative levels: the central office, the six regional offices, and the local offices—thirty-eight Community Service Areas for Social Services (CSA's) and sixty-two Welfare Service Offices for assistance payments (WSO's). The central office is organized into several offices including the Office of Assistance Payments, Office of Medical Assistance, Office of Social Services, and Office of Field Operations.

Chapter 18 of the General Laws charges DPW with the following broad responsibilities:

1. Financial assistance to those in need
2. Care and rehabilitation of the aging
3. Family and child welfare services (including foster care and adoption)
4. Social services to families and individuals, including protective, legal, homemaker, day care, sheltered work, informal education, home management training, and information and referral services
5. A program of medical care and assistance to certain residents of the Commonwealth

The central office became and has continued to be responsible for the planning, development, and implementation of department programs and policy.

The six regional offices are each headed by a regional manager responsible for monitoring, supervising, and managing the local offices, who reports directly to the associate commissioner for field operations in the central office.

The social service staff includes Information–Referral–Follow-up (IRF) workers who provide general information and referral services to the community and respond to the requests of eligible people for department services; generalist social workers; specialist social workers, including Protective Services and CHINS (Children in Need of Service); and resource mobilization workers who develop new resources and mobilize existing community resources. A family agency may apply for CHINS status with the juvenile court when a child breaks a law. This action can result in a hearing before a judge and the family, concerned agencies, and usually the Department of Youth Services become involved in the implementation of the court's decision. CSA office staff includes clerical personnel, case aides, and social service technicians.

The sixty-two local Welfare Service Offices (WSOs) in Massachusetts provide assistance payments, food stamps, and medical assistance to clients. Each WSO is administered by a director. Assistance payments staff perform two functions: intake workers determine eligibility, and ongoing workers maintain assistance payments cases.

Assistance Payments Programs

The Office of Assistance Payments consists of two major components:

Program Analysis, which is the development and promulgation of official policy on eligibility and benefit levels in Aid to Families with Dependent Children (AFDC), General Relief (GR), Supplemental Security Income (SSI), Medical Assistance (MA), and food stamps.

Operations, which establishes and revises procedures and monitors the effectiveness, efficiency and conformity with federal and state regulations of the above programs at the operational (field) level.

In addition, the quality control system and the enumeration project are run under the auspices of the Office of Assistance Payments.

Assistance payments programs include Aid to Families with Dependent Children, General Relief, Supplemental Security Income (SSI), Food Stamp Program, Child Support Program, and a Quarterly Grant for recurring household expenses.

Department of Youth Services

The Department of Youth Services (DYS) has undergone a complete reorganization within past years. In 1969 legislation was enacted that abolished the Division of Youth Service, located within the Department of Education, and established the DYS within the Executive Office of Human Services. The major responsibility of the division involved the supervision of five large institutions: the Juvenile Guidance Center in Bridgewater, the Lancaster Industrial School for Girls, Lyman School, the Residential Treatment Unit at Oakdale, and the Shirley Industrial School. These training schools had an average daily population of 850 boys and girls ages seven through eighteen.

These institutions were intended to facilitate rehabilitation, yet their regimented, impersonal life-styles left many young people antagonized and embittered toward society and themselves. Consequently, the reorganization legislation included a mandate to expand the old system of treatment with new methods that had a greater potential for success. The state subsequently embarked on a new program of deinstitutionalization: many of the state institutions, as well as the county training schools, were closed down. As they were closed, they were replaced with smaller programs at the community level—group homes, foster care homes, and nonresidential treatment programs (e.g., job training, alternative schools)—and small, secure treatment units were designed to provide individualized care in a more homelike atmosphere and to permit closer relationships between the children and the staff or foster parents.

Massachusetts Rehabilitation Commission

The Massachusetts Rehabilitation Commission (MRC), a single state agency within the Executive Office of Human Services, is charged by law with the administration of the federal/state vocational rehabilitation program. Its legislative mandate to provide vocational rehabilitation services to all eligible handicapped persons (except the blind) derives from the Rehabilitation Act of 1973 as amended and Chapter 6 of the General Laws of Massachusetts.

While the Massachusetts Rehabilitation Commission is not chartered specifically to serve a particular age or disability group, it has always served a large number of children (persons under twenty-two years of age). Statistics indicate that approximately 32 percent, or 9,770, of MRC clients are under twenty-two years of age at time of referral.

ORGANIZATION

The MRC has a central administration office, six regional offices, and thirty-four area offices. Area office counselors work with clients in the client's own communities.

The commission is divided at the central level into three divisions: Client Services, Administration and Support Services, and Disability Determination Services for SSDI (Social Security Disability Insurance)/SSI applications. While all but the Client Services Division operate at the central level, each division provides technical assistance, coordination, direction, and consultation to the area and regional office.

In order to be eligible for vocational rehabilitation services, a client must have a physical or mental disability that is a substantial handicap to employment, but he or she may reasonably be expected through vocational rehabilitation services to engage in a gainful employment. Homemaking can be considered gainful employment. Referrals are made to MRC from schools, hospitals, clinics, physicians, the Departments of Public Welfare, Public Health, and Mental Health, and other public or private agencies and organizations. Clients are also often self-referred or referred by families and friends.

During the initial interview, the area office counselor and client work together in a preliminary vocational and social assessment of the client's situation. When necessary for purposes of eligibility determination and plan development, additional medical and/or psychological diagnostic information may be acquired so as to have a complete picture of the client's situation. Information may be discussed with the area medical consultant, and the counselor makes the final decision as to eligibility. Upon completion of the diagnostic phase, the counselor and client work together to develop and implement a rehabilitation plan leading toward a suitable vocational objective.

After eligibility is determined and the client and counselor have worked out a rehabilitation program of services, counseling and guidance, which are basic to the whole rehabilitation process, continue to be provided directly by the MRC counselor. However, all other services are provided on a purchase-of-service basis. According to state law, all services other than counseling, guidance, placement, and diagnostic services are subject to a consideration of the client's financial need; in some cases, the client may be expected to pay for all or part of rehabilitation services.

Department of Mental Health

The legislated responsibilities of the Department of Mental Health, as required by the Massachusetts General Law, Chapter 19, Section 1, are described quite generally as taking "cognizance of all matters affecting the mental health of the citizens of the Commonwealth and the welfare of the mentally retarded." In addition, Chapter 19 gives the Department of Mental Health the authority, through its commissioner, to establish whatever services, departments, or facilities are needed to meet this responsibility.

ORGANIZATION

The Department of Mental Health has forty catchment areas in seven regions. Citizen participation is guaranteed through a Regional Advisory Council without statutory power in each of the seven regions, and area boards with a legislated mandate to set priorities on each of the forty catchment areas.

Administratively, the line of authority goes from the commissioner to the associate commissioner to the regional service administrator to the area director. The area director is responsible for meeting mental health and mental retardation needs within the catchment area. To fulfill this function, he or she is manager of the area service system and ultimately the in-patient unit service in his or her area.

In carrying out its responsibilities, the area board performs a number of functions:

1. Acts as the representative of area citizens
2. Advises regarding local needs in developing mental health and retardation services
3. Reviews and approves the annual plan, and reviews and makes recommendations on the annual budget for mental retardation and mental health services
4. Reviews contracted programs and services
5. Consults with the commissioner on personnel, area program priorities, admission policies, and relations with other agencies
6. Communicates with the state advisory council (of which half of the membership is from area boards)
7. Receives and administers grants or funds; receives funds under contracts
8. Holds regular and special meetings of the area board at which the president and other officers are elected annually and rules for the organization are adopted

Area boards are an essential element in the effective development and administration of community-based mental health and mental retardation services. Because their meetings are open to the public and their membership is composed of citizens from all towns in the area, they help to keep programs accountable to the local citizenry and aid in disseminating program information to the community at large.

Each year the area office is required to publish an area plan. The plan identifies mental health and retardation services available within the area. It also establishes priorities for program development for the coming fiscal year as determined by the area office and the area board. Questions concerning specific mental health and/or retardation services should always be directed to the area director. The area director clearly has responsibility for the distribution of DMH community resources and institutions located in his or her area. The area office staff also has access to information on federal and state grants and moneys available to the community for mental health and retardation services.

Area office staff include an area director, an associate director, a mental retardation coordinator, and, in some areas, a drug/

child coordinator. The other area staff are assigned in specific area programs.

Department of Public Health

The Department of Public Health, a division within the Executive Office of Human Services, is responsible for preventing disease and promoting health within the Commonwealth. To carry out these responsibilities the department is functionally organized into four major areas: health protection, health regulation, health services, and health planning.

HEALTH PROTECTION

The programs in health protection are fundamental to protecting the health of the citizens of the Commonwealth. They are programs that are performed by the state to guarantee a rapid, professional response to unusual public health threats. Such programs include setting standards for the safety and the quality of food, drugs, and consumer products; communicable and venereal disease control; specialized diagnostic laboratory services; provision of serums and vaccines; radiation control and monitoring compliance with articles I through V and X of the State Sanitary Code. The Division of Family Health Services, Local Health Services, and Preventive Medicine as well as Lead Paint Poisoning Control are also included in this area.

HEALTH REGULATION

Over the last several years the department, in response to new federal and state legislation, has substantially increased its activity in the area of health regulation. Licensure of hospitals, nursing homes, and clinics, certification of licensed facilities for participation in reimbursement of Medicare and Medicaid, the determination-of-need program, and emergency medical services are all examples of major health regulatory activities.

HEALTH SERVICES

Within the general area of health services, the department directly provides hospital-based services and alcoholism services.

These direct health services are provided through the department's seven public health hospitals and the numerous community-based programs and out-patient clinics it supports across the Commonwealth.

HEALTH PLANNING

The Department of Public Health has been federally designated as the State Health Planning and Development agency under Public Law 93-641, the National Health Planning and Resources Development Act of 1974. The Office of State Health Planning, within the Department of Public Health, is responsible for preparation of the State Health Plan, which will list statewide priorities, goals, and objectives for an integrated health care system.

Massachusetts Commission for the Blind

The Massachusetts Commission for the Blind (MCB) was established in 1906 with a legislative mandate to plan and develop programs for ameliorating the condition of the blind. In 1906, the register of the blind was established. The initial effort of the commission to establish the numbers of blind persons in the Commonwealth yielded 3,676 names.

Between 1906 and 1918, the corporate form of the commission, including an expanded body of services and programs, began to take shape.

In 1918, as part of a statewide reorganization of state departments, the commission was transferred to the Department of Education, as the Division of the Blind.

Under the guidance of several administrators until 1966, the division underwent a gradual expansion of services and programs to accommodate the increasing numbers of blind persons needing services.

The Division of the Blind was abolished in 1966 under a reorganization of the Department of Education, thus paving the way for the creation of the General Court of a new Commission for the Blind. The commission was given total autonomy of organization and operation. By now, the rehabilitation of blind persons has become far and away the top-priority goal of the agency, followed by expanding services to the elderly.

Aside from the administrative structure, which includes the commissioner, deputy commissioner, general counsel, and training office, there is also a regional, a program, and a fiscal structure. All services of the commission are now provided on a regional level. That is, the state is divided into six regions, each with a director who is accountable to the commissioner, as well as vocational rehabilitation counselors, social rehabilitation workers, and rehabilitation teachers.

The Program Department includes the following services, which are provided on a statewide basis from the Boston Office of the Commission for the Blind: Medical Assistance, Talking Book Program, Preschool Unit, Multihandicapped, Community Mobility, Bureau of Industries, Vending Facilities Program, Career Placement Office, Engineer (Equipment). The Program Department also contains the Research Unit.

Free-travel pass/identification cards are issued to legally blind persons by the Central Registration Department of the Commission for the Blind. Also available are out-of-state travel concessions from the American Foundation for the Blind.

Office for Children

OVERVIEW

The Office for Children was created by the Massachusetts Legislature in July 1972 and began statewide operations in January 1973. Chapter 785 of the Acts of 1972 mandated that the new agency be created to function as an advocate for children and to monitor and regulate the quality of children's services. Instead of directly administering services, the agency was designed to ensure that all children and their families receive the services they need. Equally important, the agency was mandated to increase the level of public participation in governmental decisions affecting children. Through a statewide network of forty-two local Councils for Children and a statewide Advisory Council, the agency has worked aggressively to involve and organize Massachusetts citizens concerned about the quality and quantity of services provided for children in the Commonwealth. As of January 1978, the agency enjoyed the affiliation of some 8,000 such citizen volunteers.

ORGANIZATION

The Office for Children operates on the local, regional, and central levels. The central office is located in Boston, regional offices in each of the seven regions of the state, and area offices in forty-two substate areas.

The functions of the office are divided into two areas: administrative and operating. The administrative components include the offices of the director and deputy director, as well as those for legal affairs, fiscal affairs, and legislative and public affairs. The operating components are Program and Community Placement and Licensing, Special Education Programs Unit (766), and Families for Foster Children. The administrative components are located at the local and regional levels.

Department of Social Services

The most recently established body within the human services is the Department of Social Services (DSS). Its first commissioner, Mary Jane England, came from the medical profession to set new direction and to administer the department. She set forward as its first priority that of providing strength to family life. In her own words: "We understand . . . that 'family life' and 'families' have been changing. As a result we are changing our services to meet new needs."

The following overview of the new department was made available to Special Education Administrators in 1981.

Chapter 552 of the General Laws as enacted by the 1978 General Court and amended in the 1979 General Court established the Department of Social Services. Beginning July 1, 1980, the legislation mandates a comprehensive program of social services at the area level accessible to all regardless of income. The boundaries of the forty areas and six regions established by DSS conform with the uniform EOHS regional and area boundaries originally set in 1977 and approved by the EOHS secretary consistent with Section 16 of Chapter 6A.

The legislature directed DSS to adapt, organize, and coordinate area-based social services to meet the needs of certain population groups, the most important of which is children and families. The Department of Social Services must provide a program of comprehensive services for

> . . . families, children and unmarried parents, which program shall, among other objectives, serve to assist, strengthen and encourage family life for the protection and care of children, assist and encourage the use by any family of all available resources to this end, and provide substitute care of children only when preventive services have failed and the family itself or the resources needed and provided to the family are unable to insure the integrity of the family and the necessary care and integrity of the family and the necessary care and protection to guarantee the rights of any child to sound health and normal physical, mental, spiritual and moral development.

The agency is further responsible for adults in need of social, legal, health, rehabilitation, employment, or other service and other population groups that require special services, such as battered women.

The legislation directs the commissioner to establish a twenty-one-member citizen board in each social service area whose role is to advise the area director in developing a responsive, relevant service system designed to address the particular concern of the individual social service areas.

Mission and Philosophy

The services mandated by state law under Chapters 18B and 119 of the General Laws focus on the family. Provision of all services is directed toward enabling adults and children to live in their own homes and with their own families. When there is a threat to the continuing integrity of the family unit, preventive services are required. When services provided have failed to support an individual at home or with the family, a greater degree of agency intervention is necessary. Such intervention should be within the least restrictive framework and consistent with the most effective services possible. If out-of-home placement of an adult or child is necessary, this should be considered an interim solution while permanent plans are developed and implemented. The agency priority will be on returning the adult or child to his or her own home if possible or to a new permanent living arrangement when services to the family unit have failed.

As of July 1, 1980, DSS assumed custody of the more than 10,000 children and youth currently in the care of Department of Public Welfare. The goals of the services to individuals and families are

- To assist, strengthen, encourage family life for the protection and care of children
- To establish/preserve independence at the highest level of functioning
- To promote the integrity and quality of family life
- To promote the individual's capacity to contribute productively to society
- To develop a permanent plan for each child in the care of the Department
- To maintain each child in the department in the least restrictive setting as close to home as possible
- To promote socialization through the creative use of leisure time

Service goals are to be accomplished through a strong, aggressive, and competent public social services program administered by the Department of Social Services. This agency is to purchase such services from other public and voluntary agencies that will complement and supplement those delivered directly by the department. These services, whether provided directly or purchased, are to be done in such a manner as to assure that the rights and dignity of individuals are maintained. This is to be done by channeling major agency efforts to access needed services, to focus on case assessment and evaluation, and to assure case accountability.

The quality of services are to be established and maintained through the promotion of high personnel standards for selection and retention of personnel within the agency and through the purchase of services from agencies with high standards. An aggressive monitoring and evaluation of direct and purchased services are intended to determine whether delivered services are meeting the agency's standards.

Training is provided to develop and enhance staff practice skills. This is facilitated through a manpower development program that aims to have an impact on all levels of staff—professional, clerical, paraprofessional—and includes individualized training plans geared toward promoting career opportunities.

Major factors in achieving maximum benefits of social services to clients while avoiding duplication of effort are to hold agency staff (department) accountable for its action, based on clearly established responsibilities. The department defines the functions of the organizational structure and individuals who are assigned to specific units.

Organizationally, the department exercises its functions through three levels—central, regional, and area offices. Each level of the agency has clearly defined responsibilities which are as follows.

AREA OFFICES

The primary responsibilities are:

- Administration of all programs of services provided via the agency
- Participation in the contracting and utilization of services purchased by the department
- Program monitoring and staff evaluation
- Recommendation of policy and program modifications
- Development of an annual area plan and budget in consultation with the area citizen board

REGIONAL OFFICES

The primary responsibilities are:

- Supervision of the administration of program of services provided via the area office
- Program monitoring and evaluation
- Staff recruitment, development, and evaluation
- Appointing authority
- Spending authority
- Recommendation of policy and program modifications

- Participation in the contracting of services purchased by the department

The primary responsibilities are:

- Establishment of mission, priorities, and goals
- Development of programs and policies
- Supervision of regional offices
- Development of standards and regulations

The area offices have primary responsibility for administering comprehensive social services in accord with the department's policy as promulgated by the commissioner. Such services are provided in accordance with the standards and guidelines that govern quality and timeliness established by the Department of Social Services.

The regional offices have primary responsibility for supervising the administration of all programs as provided through the area offices. Program evaluation and technical assistance are important functions in assuring the quality and responsiveness of the agency's services.

The central office is responsible for the development and promulgation of all official department regulations, policies, and procedures. To promote uniformity of interpretations, the central office provides technical assistance to the regional offices to ensure a consistent understanding of regulations, policies, and procedures.

Each level of the agency is responsible for monitoring and evaluating the staff, agencies, and programs that deliver social services and for making recommendations for needed modifications or new programs. Only in this way can the public be assured that the Legislative intent that created the new agency will be achieved, and only in this way can the philosophy and mission of the department deliver on the promise implicit in Chapter 552.

Human Service Delivery at Local Level

The concept of identifying those people who are to receive human service programs at the local level and having the administration located in designated area offices is an eminently sound idea—eminently sound because, if correctly carried out, it gives a greater chance of more accurate referrals and treatment plans and better public participation and support, and hence a more cost-effective system.

In 1978, the Department of Education and the Executive Office of Human Services jointly released a document entitled *Summary of Massachusetts Area Strategy*. I quote its statement of intent:

> This document summarizes the intent of Massachusetts to establish coordinated planning and management committees on the state, regional and area levels and a coordinated service delivery system within each area. At a minimum, community mental health, Title XX, rehabilitation and special education will coordinate their service delivery efforts within each area. All six regions and 40 areas have begun to develop various aspects of a coordinated system. Six areas will be advanced to demonstrate new models and evaluate the effects of coordinated services. By 1979, Massachusetts will reflect a consistent organization structure in which a high degree of coordination exists at all levels.[6]

I cannot fault this statement. Sadly, however, those who attempted to implement an area-based service delivery plan have failed abysmally. We do not, seven years later, have cooperation between agencies. We have statements of cooperation between DSS and DMH and the public schools. However, the human service agencies more often than not use their escape clause, which says, in effect, "If we have funds we will be pleased to cooperate"—and who can really blame them? They are subject to political pressures and the vagaries of the state legislature.

I believe that the reason for our failure to successfully launch a coordinated system of human service delivery is of a systemic nature. It lies in our failure to recognize that any such effort must involve both the primary service deliverers, the public schools, and the human services. Countless efforts have been made by each group working independently of the others. I believe that the only way to bring about cooperation among the schools and the agencies is through legislation. I so testified before the members of the Governor of Massachusetts Joint Education Committee in February 1984, urging their consideration for support of legislation on linkages between the public schools and the human services suggesting this be written into the comprehensive education bill that was about to go before the legislature, then known as House Bill 5000. Some of us were disappointed that strong legislation has not materialized, even though there remains a good deal of support for it.

I decided to put my energies into the launching of a pilot project involving community-based cooperative service delivery with the public schools and the human services. This plan became known as Project Link and began with a proposal I submitted to the Department of Mental Health on June 25, 1984 entitled *An Initiative For Interorganizational Linkage Between the Public Schools and the Human Service Agencies* and *A Related Plan for the Evaluation of Children's Programs*. The plan was accepted by the department's Children's Division on September 5, 1984.

History of Project Link

The first phase of the project began between September 1984 and August 1985 with the conceptualization of an idea, the choosing of a location, the establishment of a board, the development and researching of our model, and the planning for our second phase of operation. Our purpose was to set out an efficient way for our group of human service and public school professionals to deliver support services to handicapped children and their families in Newton, Massachusetts.

STATEMENT OF PROBLEM—ORIGINAL PROPOSAL

The first statement of the problem is found in the proposal made to the Department of Mental Health on June 25, 1984 as follows:

When serious concerns over a student's educational, social, or emotional well-being surface and interrupt the process of schooling, the schools and the human services do not consistently work together in an effective way. They do not jointly and consistently marshal all available resources toward a goal that guarantees children the most normal and least restrictive community-based programs possible. As jointly coordinated efforts are not commonly practiced, expensive duplication of effort exists, and children are either over tested or not tested by the appropriate professionals. Over testing results in children giving invalid responses. Under testing fails to generate needed data. Either way, children and their families fall through the inevitable cracks that then exist. The result of the lack of this early collaboration is that children are misdiagnosed and their needs go unaddressed or they are misplaced in more restrictive environments where remediation and rehabilitation are less effective or not effective at all.

The second, and directly related problem, included in the initial proposal to the Department of Mental Health states as follows:

Most child and adolescent programs are evaluated for their over-all program components exclusive of a mechanism for evaluating children's or family's individual progress. When evaluation is undertaken it is too often done separately by schools, clinics, hospitals, and human service agencies.

SELECTION OF THE BOARD OF GOVERNORS

After the basic concepts were agreed upon, the next task was to put together a board of governors, each to be highly experienced in human service and special education service delivery. In order to be productive, the board needed strong leadership. Objectivity in the three officers—chairman, director, and deputy director— was seen as being essential. All three persons needed to be motivated to develop a process for service delivery, rather than to gain funds and services for specific cases.

LOCATION OF PROJECT

Finding a location for the project took us to the office for demographic reports. These reports are very comprehensive, including all the essential details about a town's size and demographics. Ten reports on cities around Boston were reviewed. Newton was selected because of its size and location, its wide range of ethnic backgrounds, and the excellence of its public schools. The school's administrative officers were enthusiastic about the project and agreed to host it.

STATEMENT OF PROBLEM—PROJECT LINK BOARD

A discussion and reaffirmation of the problem was undertaken by the newly-formed board at its first meeting on September 5,

1984. A distillation of the board's statement is as follows: A number of barriers exist to interagency treatment planning, with some agencies having access to funding individual children's places, while others are locked into rigid standardized programs. All agencies are seen as being powerless at the local level and sometimes four levels of paperwork, are needed at each of these steps to adopt a relinking, low-cost, essential, and common-sense treatment plan. The current process of interagency collaboration was found frustrating, slow, inefficient, and bureaucratic, not serving the best interests of children and families.

An analysis of the topics most frequently surfacing in board discussion at the first meeting were:

1. The importance of nurturing ongoing dialogue that would establish a mutual trust between agencies.
2. The critical and immediate need for funds for specific areas of service delivery.
3. The importance of seeking innovative approaches to service delivery to provide better long-range planning.
4. The need for flexible funds available to break down identified structural barriers.
5. The importance of a proactive stance through preventative programs in service delivery.
6. The realization that the level of trust established and degree of collaboration attained must be upheld ultimately by a legislative mandate.
7. That twelve-month programs are needed and must become, when called for, the rule, not the exception.

These topics remained as focal points throughout Phase One of the project.

CRITERIA FOR ANALYSIS

The following criteria were identified by our panel of experts after the review of actual case studies generated in Newton.

Criteria A   Clarification of existing legislative mandates, regulations, guidelines, and public policy.

Criteria B   Structural issues and interagency agreements, process, and procedures.

Criteria C   Program issues.

RESEARCH CONCLUSION

The data taken from the children's cases where interagency collaboration was required to build treatment plans revealed that of 45 items used in the analysis, human service issues occurred 36 times, court-related issues 12, and local education authority issues 8.

PROPOSAL FOR PHASE TWO OF PROJECT LINK

The thinking, supported by our research, was that the greater degree of structure and consistency in the court system and in the regulations drawn from public laws 94–142 and 766 has resulted in fewer ambiguities, contradictions, and duplications for the schools than occur among the human service agencies. The need for multi-agency teams at the community level, each having flexible funds to build support services, became evident.

At the board's meeting on June 12, 1985, it was decided that a second phase to the project was essential. The officers of the board were to prepare an Executive Summary of the board's progress to date and to draft a statement requesting flexible funding for use in the development of treatment plans at the community level to be presented to the Secretary of the Executive Office of Human Services.

BOARD RECOMMENDATIONS—JUNE 12, 1985

We arrived at our recommendation by viewing the problem of the present overdeveloped system of service delivery conceptually. We saw four alternatives:

1. The use of highly-trained hearing officers to adjudicate between the multiple Executive Office of Human Service agencies, superimposing a new bureaucracy on an old.
2. The elimination of the bureaucratic system by staffing the Executive Office of Human Services so it could take charge and assign case managers in the field. This would represent a reversal of a historical trend that has broken down services

into more and more subtypes each becoming a large bureaucratic operation.

3. The setting up of elaborate negotiations among the agencies to work out an interagency agreement that would address the far-flung service network. This is seen as very time consuming.

4. We see the fourth alternative as being the most viable. The board has proposed that a second phase of Project Link be undertaken starting in the fall of 1985. Phase Two would continue to develop the multidisciplinary cooperative team approach at the community level. We propose a one-year pilot study that would give the local area officer of the various Executive Office of Human Services agencies autonomous and equal authority to fund collaborative treatment plans for children. Local area office directors would meet to apply funds under their control to implement therapeutic programs unencumbered by their agency's traditional limitations, and not requiring multiple levels of paper reviews. These flexible funds would come from the conversion of existing funds. The Office for Children area officer would act as a broker as each case was discussed. As treatment plans developed the officer would sign off on each plan before funds could be committed.

In the case of the applications of flexible funds being applied to a program, in contrast to an individual treatment plan, board action would be required.

Our request for flexible funding to the Executive Office of Human Services, essential for Phase Two of our project, was agreed to in June 1985. Our board can now move into Phase Two and monitor the multidisciplinary team's decisions to financially support treatment plans for children and their families in five Massachusetts communities. There is a realization on the part of Project Link board members that ultimately a legislative mandate would do much to secure our form of collaborative service delivery and achieve a firm foothold in the state.

5

The Role of the Psychiatric Consultant in Special Education

by Robert Mignone, M.D.

As a psychiatric consultant to schools, I began to visit classrooms, teachers' rooms, and counselors' offices with a sense of being a fish out of water. My traditional medical identity had always had me on hospital wards, in emergency rooms, or in consultation offices. In elementary schools, the small-scale chairs and tables, low water bubblers, and displays of crayon artwork vividly created an immediate sense of the world of little people. Visiting their classrooms and watching them shift from structured exercises, to free play, to cookie break, to playground, has given me a direct sense of the shifting requirements of their self-control and attentiveness and their social interactive skills with peers and teachers. Talking with principals and teachers directly has allowed me firsthand acquaintance with the leadership and teaching processes.

The junior high has been a fluctuating picture of "children" at times acting like young adults and at times appearing to be boys and girls. The high school is a bustle of industriousness, an achievement-oriented culture concerned also with those citizens who seem unable or unwilling to compete or produce. This preadult world reflects much of the community of both groups, for better and for worse.

My consultative role evolved into several activities: (1) discussing classroom dynamics, including teacher–student issues, (2) developing techniques for individual management problems, (3) contributing to the overall educational plan of troubled children who are learning and/or emotionally disabled (this usually includes interviewing parents so as to arrive at diagnostic understanding), (4) consulting with parents as the interface in what can become an adversary process, (5) testifying in adversary hearings regarding the psychiatric and neuromedical aspects of the educational plan, and (6) consulting with counselors in crisis situations.

Discussing Classroom Dynamics

Relationships among students and between student and teacher operate on two levels: the actual, realistic way the parties behave, and distortions based upon reminders of family relationships. For example, a given teacher behaving consistently with a group of students may be perceived by most students in a positive way, but by one as too critical, by another as too controlling, by another as not helpful enough, by another as unfair. Teachers and principals must be able to determine whether the trouble lies with themselves or with the child who is playing out some family issues. In my discussions with teachers, they have found it useful, at times crucial, to sort this out in order to resume an effective role. It has also been helpful to teachers to discern the same two dimensions in peer relationships, where, for example, some children may be playing out of family sibling rivalries or jealousies.

A case in point is Mary, a nine-year-old who had always been pleasant and cooperative in school. Then the classroom teacher, Mrs. S., noted a change during the first two semesters of the school year: Mary had become increasingly in need of guidance and support. She seemed less industrious and self-sufficient than previous teachers had described. At times she was quarrelsome and appeared to dislike the teacher. Mrs. S. had perceived herself to be generally liked by her students. Although she admittedly was having a difficult year herself personally and was feeling depleted, she wasn't sure if this was "rubbing off" on Mary or whether it was Mary who was in difficulty. Some initial questioning of the girl yielded no obvious answers. Psychiatric consultation with Mary, Mrs. S., and Mary's parents revealed that Mary's grandmother had developed cancer. Mary adored her grandmother, who had always taken a large portion of responsibility for Mary, as her mother and father both worked. She was a nurturing, caring, and supportive figure. With the onset of her illness, she was now limited in her support of Mary. The mother was not only working but also caring for the grandmother. Mary, although not directly aware of it, was feeling lost in the shuffle and unwittingly played out this family situation with her teacher in her school "family." Once she understood this, Mrs. S. was relieved to feel on track and was able to provide some extra support for Mary. The school psychologist helped Mary work through her grief and anger in play therapy so that she needed to express it less in the classroom. The principal was pleased to see his distressed student, teacher, and family making progress.

Developing Management Techniques

From time to time usual practice seems to fail in certain class-room situations. Often, however, discussions with teachers reveal that their technique or approach is not the problem. Rather, it may be a matter of accepting some unpleasant or "inappropriate" feelings such as anger, dislike, helplessness, and impotence. When these are openly discussed, especially in a group of involved personnel (classroom teacher, learning disabilities teacher, counselor, principal), it becomes possible to get unstuck and do what can realistically be done. In fact, in many instances there is only so much that can be done. Such partiality must be tolerated. This can be especially difficult when the parents underestimate the degree of the problem, blame one or more teachers, and demand more effort. All parties need to understand the role of denial and scape-goating, which overlays the pain of those involved.

On occasion, a principal has wanted to discuss the management of discipline of a particular student, especially when parents appear to be undermining the effort. It may be enough to explain to the parents about consistency of limits, positive as well as negative reinforcement, and the realities of tolerances in the school setting. However, some parents remain unwittingly exasperating in aiding and abetting the defiance or acting up. Referral to family therapy can be made.

Contributing to the Educational Plan

A child who is having difficulty learning can be evaluated from several points of view so as to devise an educational plan tailored to his or her needs. The psychiatric consultant is asked to determine what role, if any, emotional and/or neuromedical factors are playing. A most common problem in that regard is distractibility or hyperkinesis (excessive mobility). Firsthand observations in the structured classroom, the unstructured playground, and the cafeteria are important in diagnosis. Additionally, getting a developmental history from parents is essential. A view at a given point in time is not sufficient and can be misleading. For example, there is the picture of a highly distractible third-grader who moves about, talks with peers, appears unable to concentrate on prolonged tasks, is irritable, and at times has angry outbursts. It may be the first year the school system has known this boy. Only when a history from the parents reveals that he was a difficult infant with colic, was a fitful sleeper, cried often, and early on climbed out of his crib and was off and crawling or running, does the likelihood of medical hyperactivity appear. Moreover, it is heightened when further history describes his being such a "holy terror" in supermarkets, restaurants, and church that his mother had to resort to a harness by the time he was three or four. In sum, parents usually describe a characteristic story with a knowing sigh. For these children a twofold approach is needed: medication (such as Ritalin) and counseling about the impact on self-esteem. Hyperactive, distractible children have for years suffered from the criticism and exasperation of everyone around them. It is not surprising that they consider themselves "weird" and defective. This is exaggerated by taking the "nerve pill" or the "hyper pill" from the school nurse. School counselors work with these students in play therapy and group therapy. Psychiatric consultants assist with supervision when needed.

If, by contrast, the reason for distractibility is primarily emotional, the underlying issues must be clarified and help offered, either by school counselors or by referral to individual or family psychotherapy. Interviews with parents can at times be delicate, especially in terms of confidentiality. All investigative materials and impressions by psychiatric consultant and school psychologists are confidential, and only those aspects directly relevant to educational planning are disclosed, and then with the express permission of parents. Furthermore, there is always an option to exclude specific material from entering the team considerations at all. This professional stance must be firm and never give way to conflict of alliance (school versus parent). Clinical responsibility of privilege is the ultimate and fail-safe consideration.

Preventing Conflict between Parents and Staff

Disagreements between parents and educators often arise over which plan is most advisable—for example, out-of-school placement versus in-system special class, or mainstream classroom versus special classroom. Sometimes the differences can be lessened with communication so as to inform or educate. For example, if a parent is told in detail what the pros and cons are for various options, the most advisable move can be seen to be self-evident. Unfortunately, the move is usually not too easy.

Contributions to polarization can come from both sides, especially as mutual resentment and sense of impotence escalate. Typically, the educational team is armed with batteries of tests, knows just what its special programs provide, and feels confident. It knows what is best for the student. On the other hand, the unhappy parents, backed by a local advocate, point to the prior years of failure by the school system and demand a change to a private special-education school.

The tendency to blame the bearer of bad tidings is common when parents feel overwhelmed and even guilty about their child's problem. They wish they could see something hopeful, something new. They also may need to play down the nature and degree of their child's disturbance. They may need to see the trouble as neuromedical rather than psychological, or vice versa, even in the face of a thorough evaluation.

In such instances the psychiatric consultant tries to flesh out such underlying issues of denial, scapegoating, impotence, and magical thinking. He or she attempts to forge an alliance, given that all parties are interested in the child's welfare. The facts are clarified, and where differences arise, the consultant tries to see whether they are legitimate factual ones or arise from a wish not to face facts.

Take the case of Johnny L., whose hyperactive behavior and inattention had been repeatedly described to his mother by teachers and principals ever since his nursery-school days. Mrs. L. became increasingly worried and angry with her son and felt increasingly impotent as a "failed" mother. Sometimes she would share with teachers and counselors her frustrations and pain; at other times she would appear to be on a campaign against the school system, which she felt had never done enough for her son. She decried the teachers and some aspects of the program. She thought private placement through Chapter 766 was justified, and was supported in this by a local advocate. The consultation with Mrs. L., the teachers, and the school counselor was aimed at first clarifying the actual educational parameters in a concrete way so as to determine the points of disagreement. This effort served to distinguish between fact and opinion, possible and impossible. All parties needed the opportunity to become aligned around what was possible. The feelings of frustration and distress were felt by all and thereby lifted from the adversary dispute. In effect, the power conflict and scapegoating were converted into a collaborative discussion, even though it was not entirely congenial.

Testifying at Hearings

When the adversary process results in a stalemate, the matter is brought to a hearing. Psychiatric opinion is obtained regarding psychological and neuromedical aspects of the learning difficulty. Recommendation for types of programs are sought. This is straightforward testimony. There is no opportunity to mediate or facilitate as might have existed before the hearing.

Consulting with Counselors in Crisis Situations

Upon occasion a very distressed student is presented to a school psychologist or guidance counselor as suicidal. The consulting psychiatrist is available immediately by phone to assist the counselor with assessment and/or to see the student. Other clinical situations arising in school include the psychoses and acute, repeated drug and alcohol abuse. The consultant can refer to mental health professionals or directly hospitalize the disturbed child or teenager.

In my ten years of consulting to school systems, it has become clear that the psychiatrist has a definite role to play. It varies according to the situation and includes interpreter of neuromedical information, liaison between neuromedical and/or psychiatric examiners and school personnel, facilitator for parents and staff, direct diagnostician of troubled children, supervisor of school counselors, and more. After one adjusts to being in "strange territory" and gets past the disorientation of being in a little people's world, one can "dig in" and become part of the team.

Schools find it hard to get the attention of hospitals and once they do to get their point of view listened to. I have learned that schools, just like parents, have exclusive and important information to share with doctors about children. I would like to think that I have, at least in a limited number of hospitals in the Greater Boston area, convinced my colleagues of the importance of schools in the development of the mental health of children. I believe in the multidisciplinary team approach when serious mental health issues arise—that is, doctors, schools, parents, and human service personnel working together for the well-being of children. For example: A Building Planning and Placement Team reports a child's behavior. These observations are interpreted by a consultant psychiatrist, who talks with parents and suggests they consult their pediatrician as to the possibility of medication. The physician then becomes dependent upon the school to report regularly on the daily observed behavior of the student. Then and only then can a physician regulate the medication so that it will be of greatest benefit to the child. This close teamwork exemplifies for me the *modus operandi* for the next decade; it is one that I support and intend to cultivate, for I have seen it can make a significant difference in the lives of special-needs children and their families.

6
The Special-Education Appeals Process

by Arthur Murphy, Esq.

The federal special-education law, the Education for All Handi-capped Children Act,[1] offers financial incentive to all states that comply with its terms. Consistent with the purposes of the act— to prevent the unnecessary stigmatization of handicapped children, to address the individual special-educational needs of each handicapped child, and to provide every handicapped child with an appropriate education regardless of the severity of handicap— federal law requires every state receiving financial assistance to establish a network of procedural safeguards designed to protect the rights of handicapped children and their parents.[2] Among these procedural safeguards, states must guarantee parents an opportunity for an impartial due-process hearing "with respect to any matter relating to the identification, evaluation or educational placement" of a handicapped child.[3]

Subsequent to the identification of a handicapped child, a local educational agency must convene a placement team, upon which the parents have the right to serve. The functions of the placement team are to evaluate the special needs of the child and to devise an appropriate individualized education program to meet these needs.[4] In most cases, the parent and the school are able to reach an agreement as to the proper educational placement for the child.[5] When, however, such an agreement does not materialize, the law requires that an impartial hearing officer resolve any issue relating to the identification, evaluation, or placement of a handicapped child, including diagnosis of the child, content of the child's appropriate education program, and financial responsibility of the respective parties.[6]

The regulations promulgated by the Department of Education for implementing the act permit either the parents or the public educational agency to initiate a due-process hearing.[7] Once a party requests a due-process hearing with respect to a child's educational placement, however, states differ in their approach for administratively reviewing such requests. Some state laws mandate administrative review by both the local and state educational agencies, while others specify review solely by the state agency.[8] Under either procedure, no employee directly involved in the education or care of a handicapped child may conduct such a hearing.[9]

The law also furnishes the parties to a hearing with a number of due-process rights. For example, before the hearing, the educational agency must inform indigent parents of the availability and location of low-cost legal assistance or other relevant services.[10] In addition, by prohibiting certain categories of persons from conducting hearings, the law seeks to ensure that a hearing officer will truly be impartial.[11] Moreover, during the hearing a party has the right to be advised by legal counsel and by experts familiar with the child's handicap, to present evidence, to prohibit the introduction at the hearing of any evidence that the opposing party has not disclosed at least five days prior to the hearing, and to confront, cross-examine, and compel the attendance of witnesses.[12]

Because a special-education hearing is an administrative rather than a judicial proceeding, the hearing officer will not normally adhere to the formal rules of evidence.[13] This relaxation in protocol recognizes the fact-finding rather than adversarial nature of special-education appeals. In fact, the only evidence that is not admissible at the hearing is irrelevant or repetitive evidence.[14]

As a general rule the petitioner or moving party presents its case first. Although the moving party is usually a parent who has rejected the education plan proposed by the public school, in some instances, such as where public school officials desire to bring back a handicapped child from a private placement, the petitioner may be the local education agency. At the close of the presentation of evidence, both parties have a chance to summarize their cases by making closing arguments. Often, either in addition to or in lieu of closing argument, the parties submit written memoranda in support of their respective positions.

Because the opportunity for special-education placement appeals arises from the mandate to provide handicapped children with a "free appropriate public education," the fundamental consideration in any such appeal focuses upon the best interests of the handicapped child.[15] Consequently, the burden of proof during the hearing is on each party to demonstrate that its proposed placement is appropriate.[16] In this regard, however, when confronted with two appropriate programs, the law requires that a hearing officer select that placement which occurs in the least restrictive environment.[17] Significantly, if neither party proposes an appropriate program, the hearing officer has substantial latitude to modify the proposals or to choose an alternative placement that neither party has proposed.[18]

At the conclusion of a special-education appeal, a hearing officer must issue a timely written decision.[19] The hearing officer must make detailed findings of fact, as well as relevant conclusions of law, which support his or her decision.[20] Each party to the hearing has the right to receive the written decision and, upon request, to obtain a written or electronic verbatim record of the hearing.[21]

A hearing officer's decision is final, unless one of the parties to the hearing appeals the decision.[22] In states that have adopted a two-tiered appeals process,[23] a party aggrieved by the findings and decision of the local agency may appeal to the state educational agency.[24] Similarly, any party aggrieved by a decision of the state agency has the right to commence a civil action for judicial review either in state court or in federal district court.[25] Significantly, because the procedural provisions of the federal law supersede conflicting state procedures,[26] an appeal of the agency decision to court invokes a party's right under federal law to a *de novo* review.[27] During court appeals, therefore, the parties have the right to present additional evidence.[28]

On judicial review, the court makes an independent determination, based upon the preponderance of the evidence, concerning the child's appropriate educational placement. Accordingly, the court need not defer to the decision of the administrative agency.[29] In this manner, Congress has placed ultimate responsibility upon the courts for ensuring that a handicapped child receives an appropriate education.[30]

The chapter has provided an overview of the special-education placement appeals process. Obviously, when resolution of an appeal requires both administrative and judicial review, this process can become unwieldy and protracted. In addition, during an appeal the focus may tend to shift away from the needs of the handicapped child to the legal issues surrounding the placement dispute. Consequently, in an effort to minimize the need for appeals, parents and public schools should strive for flexibility and cooperation in their approach to developing a child's individualized education program.[31] Nevertheless, where agreement among the parties is impossible, the provisions for administrative and judicial review present an equitable manner of resolving differences while simultaneously enforcing a handicapped child's right to a free appropriate public education.

7
Issues in Special-Education Law

by Arthur Murphy, Esq.

Since the promulgation of the Education for All Handicapped Children Act in 1975, state and federal courts have been asked to resolve an increasing number of disputes concerning the education of handicapped children. Predictably, most of these cases involve merely factual disputes over whether the public school is capable of providing a free appropriate education. In contrast, several important legal issues surrounding the education of the handicapped have emerged. Inasmuch as they contribute significantly to defining the rights of handicapped children, as well as the responsibilities of local education agencies, these issues merit some discussion.

One common issue arising in disputes between parents and public schools is a change in a child's educational placement during the appeals process. Frequently, parents who are dissatisfied with the public school's proposed program unilaterally remove their child from the public school setting, pending administrative and judicial review, and place the child in a private day or residential school.[1] Accordingly, one of the questions for the court to answer during the ensuing appeal is which party should bear financial responsibility for the private placement.[2]

Courts have disagreed in resolving this question: some hold that parents may not retroactively recover the costs of unilateral placements,[3] while others permit reimbursement for appropriate placements when the public school has initially failed to designate an adequate program.[4] Significantly, much of the confusion surrounding the availability of retroactive reimbursement focuses upon an interpretation of part of the federal law which states:

> During the pending of any proceedings conducted pursuant to this section, unless the state or local educational agency and the parent or guardian otherwise agree, the child shall remain in the then current educational placement of such child . . . until all such proceedings have been completed.[5]

Some courts interpret this provision literally, finding that the statutory language imposes a *duty* upon parents who request due-process hearings to maintain their child's current educational placement pending administrative and judicial review.[6] Moreover, one court has observed that any violation of the duty to preserve a child's educational placement "negates any right on the part of the parents . . . to elect unilaterally to place their child in private school and recover the tuition costs thus incurred."[7] In reaching its decision that the parents' unilateral placement of the child pending appeal barred recovery of reimbursement, the court reasoned that congressional intent underlying the act mandated preservation of the status quo during any administrative or judicial proceeding.[8]

In contrast, other courts permit parents to recover retroactive reimbursement when a court ultimately finds the parents' choice of placement to be appropriate for their child.[9] Courts reaching this conclusion have variously theorized that retroactive reimbursement was proper because the public school failed initially to meet its statutory obligation to provide an appropriate education,[10] or because a favorable state agency decision has "agreed" with the parents' proposed placement,[11] or because a unilateral change in placement was necessary for health and safety as well as educational reasons.[12]

Courts will continue to disagree on questions concerning the availability of reimbursement for unilateral changes in placement.[13] Significantly, the provisions of the act neither expressly preclude nor approve reimbursement for changes in a child's placement.[14] In addition, courts recognize that the act serves as a compromise that balances budgetary constraints facing local communities against the right of handicapped children to receive appropriate educational services.[15] Consequently, it would appear that a flexible approach—which permits reimbursement in appropriate circumstances where the detriment to the child outweighs the public school's interest in preserving placement pending appeal—would best promote the discernible policy of the act.

A second important issue revolves around a determination of "related services" to which a child in need of special education is entitled. The term "related services" comprehends a wide variety of developmental, corrective, and other supportive services, including speech pathology and audiology, psychological services, physical and occupational therapy, recreation, and medical and counseling services.[16] The obligation of a local education agency to provide related services, however, arises only when a handicapped child requires such services in order "to benefit from special education."[17] Accordingly, in order to qualify for receipt of related services, a child must demonstrate educational reasons, such as inability to progress, for requiring such services.[18]

Although the drafters of the act—by requiring a nexus between special education and a child's need for related services—may have intended to recognize economic constraints that limit the ability of public schools to provide education for the handicapped, the judicial trend has been to favor requests by parents for related services rather than to protect legitimate economic interests of school committees. Courts have been unable to separate educational from noneducational needs for related services, especially when dealing with severely handicapped children.[19] Indeed, this unseverability of educational and noneducational needs may serve as the very basis for approving a parental request for related services.[20] Additionally, a court may be willing to endorse the provision of related services, although not related to education, where merely attending classes would be impossible without such services.[21]

Nevertheless, it is arguable that the courts have overly expanded the burden that Congress intended public schools to bear in providing handicapped children with an appropriate education. Not only are courts reluctant to deny requests for related services, owing to their refusal or inability to isolate a child's noneducational needs, but courts also require schools to provide services that appear to be outside the scope of the statutory definition. For example, almost all of the courts considering the question have ruled that federal law requires the provision of "psychotherapy" as a related service.[22] As commentators have observed, however, the act seems to prohibit public delivery of psychotherapy inasmuch as it neither contemplates the provision of services by psychiatrists nor includes "therapy" in the enumeration of available psychological services.[23] Accordingly, instead of deferring to parental requests for related services, courts should devise a more equitable formula for allocating responsibility in questionable cases.[24]

Another troubling question for the courts has been whether schools should have the authority to impose discipline upon handicapped children. In 1975 the United States Supreme Court established minimum due-process guarantees to which public school officials must adhere before suspending or expelling students.[25] The Court recognized that even when imposing short-term suspensions, the school must give a child prior notice and an opportunity to be heard.[26] Furthermore, the Court stated that for long-term suspensions or expulsions, more formal procedures, such as the opportunity to secure counsel or call and confront witness, may be required.[27]

Courts agree that handicapped children are not immune to disciplinary sanctions, "nor are they entitled to participate in programs when their behavior impairs the education of other children in the program.[28] In addition, courts acknowledge that minimum due-process protections are sufficient when imposing short-term suspensions upon handicapped children.[29] When school officials contemplate the imposition of long-term suspensions or expulsions for handicapped children, however, it may be necessary to follow the change-in-placement provisions of the act, including parental notification and consent, opportunity for reevaluation, and opportunity for a hearing.[30]

In long-term suspension cases, courts require schools to resort to the procedural safeguards of the act because such sanctions constitute substantial changes in a child's educational placement.[31] Judicial recognition that handicapped children deserve greater protection, however, should not prevent a school system from utilizing the same disciplinary procedures used with nonhandicapped children when the child's behavior bears no relation to his or her handicap.[32] In this situation, there is no reason why a handicapped child should be treated differently from other children. In any event, it is apparent that when administrators are considering discipline for a handicapped child, they should convene a meeting of persons familiar with the child in order to determine whether the child's behavior is related to his or her handicap and whether a different program must be considered and offered.[33] Significantly, even where long-term suspension or expulsion is appropriate, it may be necessary to provide some other form of educational services so that the sanction does not deny the handicapped student a "free appropriate public education."[34]

Finally, much confusion has emerged as a result of judicial efforts to define the term "appropriate education." The act contains only a broad definition of the term, stating that it is

> special education and related services which (A) Have been provided at public expense, under public supervision, and without charge, (B) Meet the standards of the State educational agency, . . . and (D) Are provided in conformity with the individualized educational program. . . .[35]

Some courts construe this provision to mean that the definition of the term varies with the establishment by individual states of educational and programmatic standards.[36] Under this approach, then, any program that met these standards would be "appropriate," so long as it was free and provided to meet individual needs.[37] In addition, a court could only review state standards to ensure that their compliance comported with the overall policies of the act.[38]

In contrast, other courts have attempted to formulate their own definition of "appropriate education." Noting that the failure of the act to define the term precisely has led to diverse results, several courts have recently concurred that

> An "appropriate education" could mean an "adequate" education— that is, an education substantial enough to facilitate a child's progress from one grade to another and to enable him or her to earn a high

school diploma. An "appropriate education" could also mean one which enables the handicapped child to achieve his or her full potential. Between these two extremes, however, is a standard which . . . is more in keeping with the regulations, with the Equal Protection decisions which motivated the passage of the Act, and with common sense. This standard would require that each handicapped child be given the opportunity to achieve his full potential commensurate with the opportunity provided to other children.[39]

As one court has observed, this standard "provides the handicapped child with the opportunity to achieve her full potential but takes into account that such a task is equally fair and feasible only to the extent that such opportunity must be commensurate with the opportunity granted to nonhandicapped in the same system."[40]

Significantly, this latter standard recognizes that a school system has the obligation neither to provide the "best" possible education program nor to "maximize" a child's learning potential.[41] Rather, it is essential only that local education agencies provide handicapped and nonhandicapped children with equal education opportunity. Nevertheless, application of this definition of "appropriate education" has produced apparently contradictory rulings. In one case, for example, where a court ordered a public school to provide a full-time sign language interpreter for a hearing-impaired child, the standard seemed to require delivery of the "best" program.[42] Another court, however, relied upon the standard in finding a public school program to be appropriate for a deaf child, despite clear recognition that the program was not the "best" available for the child.[43] Perhaps because of the imprecision of this definition or the potential impact upon special education produced by judicial application of varying definitions of "appropriateness," the U.S. Supreme Court is currently reviewing the New York case that developed the definition.[44] Consequently, within the near future, courts and educators alike may be able to determine with certainty whether a particular program is appropriate. Ultimately, any uniform standard of "appropriateness" should balance competing interests by recognizing not only the best interests of handicapped children but also the monetary restrictions placed upon local school systems.

Such are the varying and complex nature of issues that may arise in special education placement disputes. Because each state has devised its own special-education laws, inconsistencies in judicial resolution of these issues are inevitable. Moreover, diversity in judicial results may stem from the difficulty of balancing competing public school and parental interests. Regardless of benefits or detriments, however, it is apparent that legislative recognition of the rights of handicapped children to an appropriate public education has placed a considerable burden upon the courts to oversee the broad area of special education.

8
Matthew v. A School System in Massachusetts

This chapter tells how a special-education team upheld the Public Law Chapter 766 and its basic tenet that all children must receive adequate and appropriate programs in the least restrictive settings. It is necessary to bring this information to the fore lest we lose sight of one of the most important underlying concepts of the law. The contents of a special-education appeals hearing is reported on these pages with the full cooperation and permission of the parents of the child in the case. I admire the determination and courage of Matthew's parents in their willingness to smooth the way for other handicapped children in the future, thus ensuring that their rights will be upheld under the law.

Background

Matthew started his education at the age of four, entering an early-childhood program that was well established as an integral part of a regular neighborhood school.

Because Matthew was a Down's syndrome child, his individualized educational plan included speech therapy, occupational therapy, counseling support, and special help from a learning disabilities specialist. At the age of seven, Matthew changed programs and joined another established program in a school to which all his peers moved at fourth grade. He continued to receive all the special services, and most of his therapists continued with him at the new school. Matthew continued to make steady progress. His parents were very supportive and were active participants in the team process. By the time he reached age nine, the specialists reported that

93

in language development he demonstrated ability to understand and respond functionally to spoken language at the four- to six-year level, and when sign language was combined with the spoken word Matthew was able to identify fourteen out of fifteen items shown to him. Matthew's psychologist noted definite strengths in his social functioning and his ability to control his environment. His learning-disabilities specialist reported that he had progressed to a point where he was functioning between three years and five and a half years developmentally. The occupational therapist saw remarkable growth in adaptive skills of daily living. She said he was able to work with a moderate amount of supervision.

The Building Planning and Placement Team, in updating his individual educational plan at age nine, felt confident that on balance steady progress was being realized and that his program delivery should remain substantially the same. However, the team's position was challenged by the superintendent of schools, who had decided that an outside placement should be found for Matthew and, while that was being accomplished, that it would be sufficient for him to be served by a teacher of aide status rather than a qualified teacher.

Mental retardation and Down's syndrome in particular especially interested certain members of the team who realized that little was known about the effect that regular school programs had upon mainstreamed Down's syndrome children. The recorded research done on Down's syndrome began with J. Langdon Down, an Englishman, in 1867. Further research in 1959 clearly established that Down's syndrome was caused by the presence of an extra chromosome—forty-seven instead of forty-six.[1] Then, in 1960, studies of Down's syndrome adults and children suggested that institutionalized populations may average from five to ten points less in their intelligence quotients than those living at home.[2] In 1970 research showed that among Down's syndrome people without cardiac abnormalities from age five to fifty, life expectancy is only about 6 percent below normal and not different from that of other persons with similar degrees of retardation.[3]

With a knowledge that a supportive home environment could produce healthy growth for Down's syndrome children, and knowing that Matthew had a sound heart, Matthew's support team considered it professionally appropriate to take the position that he should remain in the least restrictive environment, namely his home school, and be taught by a qualified teacher and be given therapy by the support team.

The parents rejected Matthew's individual education plan in September 1983 because permission to rehire his teacher had been refused and an aide was to be put in that place. The Bureau of Special Education Appeals held a prehearing on November 1, 1983, and following that, the hearing officer issued an interim order stating (1) that Matthew's program should be a 502.4 prototype,[4] (2) that the types of services outlined in the current individual educational plan are appropriate to meet Matthew's needs, (3) that Matthew should be taught by a qualified teacher who is certified in severe special needs, and (4) that Matthew is not being taught by a teacher with the foregoing qualifications and that a qualified teacher should be found immediately.

The Hearing

The hearing was declared open at 9:30 A.M., December 16, 1983, by the hearing officer. He swore in the witnesses for the school and for the parents. The hearing officer made an opening statement and called upon the attorney for the school to make her opening statement and call her first witness. The testimony was then given, followed by a cross-examination by the parents' attorney. This procedure continued with all witnesses, interrupted only when the hearing officer felt the need for clarification on a given point. The attorney for the parents was then invited to give her opening statement and call her witnesses, and the school's attorney was allowed to cross-examine each witness. At the conclusion of this, the hearing officer called for closing statements, first from the attorney for the parents and then from the attorney for the schools. The session was closed by the hearing officer's statement that he would render a decision within twenty-five working days.

The following transcript is taken from an audiotape made by the hearing officer at the time of the hearing—all last names have been deleted. This transcript was submitted to both lawyers for their review.

HEARING OFFICER: This is the case of Matthew and a Massachusetts Public School System. The School System has legal representation as do the parents. Both Attorneys are experienced with 766 and 94-142 matters and I will ask that you waive an opening statement by the Hearing Officer.

ATTORNEYS: We agree.

HEARING OFFICER: In a prehearing conference, the parties reached agreement—Matthew's diagnosis is correct and his 1982–83 Individualized Educational Plan is adequate and appropriate to meet his special needs and that the general goals and objectives on the 1983–84 Individualized Educational Plan are appropriately stated. The main question we are dealing with is the specific setting where Matthew's program can be implemented adequately and appropriately, consistent with the Law. Attorneys, please limit your questions to the parameter of the stipulation. I will ask everyone starting on my left to please state their name for the record and I will swear you in as witnesses collectively.

SCHOOL WITNESSES: Identified themselves: School Psychologist, Occupational Therapist, Speech Pathologist, Director of Special Education.

PARENTS' WITNESSES: Matthew's mother and father and his former special needs teacher.

HEARING OFFICER: Do you all swear that the testimony you are about to give will be the whole truth?

WITNESSES: We do.

School System Attorney's Opening Statement

It is the School Committee's position that Matthew does indeed have an adequate and appropriate plan, as written. The goals and objectives are appropriate for him. The question is where is he to be taught. It is our position that Matthew should be taught outside of his home School System in a private school program which has been identified. We believe that this school has many of the services that would meet the needs as identified. We have complied with the interim order of the hearing officer by doing as directed, first, hiring a person who is qualified to teach Matthew within his home town. This is on an interim basis pursuant to your order. Second, the Department of Special Education has engaged in an extensive search for programs in other public schools as well as private locations for Matthew. You will hear testimony on the pros and cons of these schools.

HEARING OFFICER: Would you present your first witness.

SCHOOL SYSTEM ATTORNEY: State your name and position for the record.

WITNESS: I hold the position of Director of Pupil Personnel Services and have done so for the past 8½ years.

SCHOOL SYSTEM ATTORNEY: Please tell us about your background.

DIRECTOR OF SPECIAL EDUCATION: I hold a B.A. in political science and an M.A. in education and psychology. I earned an associateship in child psychology from London University in 1972. I am certified as school principal, superintendent, administrator of special education and have had clinical and teaching experience from kindergarten through graduate school.

ATTORNEY FOR SCHOOL: Do you know Matthew?

DIRECTOR OF SPECIAL EDUCATION: Yes, I do. His program takes place in the same building where I have my office.

SCHOOL SYSTEM ATTORNEY: You heard the stipulations we entered into prior to this hearing—are they correct?

DIRECTOR OF SPECIAL EDUCATION: Yes, they are correct.

SCHOOL SYSTEM ATTORNEY: There was one stipulation regarding diagnoses of Matthew's needs and his need for a total communicative setting. Do you recall this?

DIRECTOR OF SPECIAL EDUCATION: Yes, I do. I have consulted with the professionals on Matthew's team and agree with them that a total communication approach is appropriate for him.

SCHOOL SYSTEM ATTORNEY: One other item I would like to draw your attention to—do you agree that Matt is a very social person?

DIRECTOR OF SPECIAL EDUCATION: Yes, I would. Sometimes too social, in the sense that when he comes to visit in my office he wants to stay and make phone calls. He communicates very effectively for a nonverbal child. I don't have command of sign language, but I find communication quite easy, and since he has had tubes placed in his ears, his speech is becoming much more intelligible. He communicates with many adults around the school using sign language.

SCHOOL SYSTEM ATTORNEY: Could you state the school committee's position on two matters. First, the placement and secondly, whether or not the interim order has been complied with.

DIRECTOR OF SPECIAL EDUCATION: I will take up the latter point first. I feel we have done a complete job of complying with the order. We contacted four special needs collaboratives and several public and private schools. I was unable to accompany the team members on all visits because of the pressure of work. However, the team supplied me with written reports upon the completion of all site visits for a total of six visits.

SCHOOL SYSTEM ATTORNEY: We have the letters you wrote to the collaboratives.

DIRECTOR OF SPECIAL EDUCATION: Yes, the private school, thought to be the most likely to meet his needs, did seem to me to meet the objectives of his Individual Educational Plan with some exceptions that the team noted, including the nature of this school's population, which was all handicapped, developmentally delayed, and behaviorally disturbed. The second part of your question: would I clarify the Superintendent and School Committee's position: I can best do this by reading from a memo dated September 6, 1983, from Superintendent to the Director of Pupil Personnel Services as follows: third paragraph reads, "I have been in contact with the Director of the Regional Education Center to question whether we would be responsible for providing one teacher for one child. She believes that the state would not require that or expect a school system to assume such a financial burden, particularly when there was and is another option." It goes on to direct my team to explore other options for placement, options that in fact we did explore and found inappropriate for Matthew.

HEARING OFFICER: No one is proposing these other options.

SCHOOL SYSTEM ATTORNEY: They are probably included in the Record.

DIRECTOR OF SPECIAL EDUCATION: The other thing that helps clarify the position of the school district is my review of the case with the School Committee. I am quoted in their minutes as saying that Matthew's present Individual Educational Plan calls for a full-time qualified teacher. He presently has been provided with an aide only, and the parents feel we should follow his plan and provide a teacher. The consensus of the School Committee was that we should continue on to an appeals hearing in the case in the meantime and seek alternative programs that would meet the child's needs in a more economical way. This then is the position of the School Committee and the Superintendent of Schools. I was asked to state this position at the hearings.

SCHOOL SYSTEM ATTORNEY: Did the school system take any steps to hire a person to teach Matthew on an interim basis?

DIRECTOR OF SPECIAL EDUCATION: Yes. I will refer to another memorandum dated October 1983 from the Superintendent to me. "I am in receipt of your memo requesting that we adhere to the Hearings Officer's directive to provide Matthew with a teacher. It is my understanding that we have no choice in that situation so your recommendation is accepted. However, I must remind you of the School Committee's recommendation to you that you strive diligently to find an acceptable, appropriate as well as cost effective program for that youngster. I do not consider one teacher/one child as truly cost effective to our school district." Then, having received that "green light," I proceeded to take the necessary steps to hire the teacher. We advertised, screened and interviewed teachers, and I have selected a teacher who we feel is qualified. I have just learned by phone moments before this hearing that said teacher has been approved as Matthew's teacher by the School Committee.

SCHOOL SYSTEM ATTORNEY: You are comfortable that on an interim basis Matthew could receive an adequate and appropriate program at his home school?

DIRECTOR OF SPECIAL EDUCATION: Yes. I am comfortable and professionally confident that Matthew's Individual Educational Plan can be implemented and that newly identified needs due to his improved hearing after his operation can be met.

SCHOOL SYSTEM ATTORNEY: Is there anything else you would care to add about the School Committee's position or anything else?

DIRECTOR OF SPECIAL EDUCATION: No.

Cross-Examination of Director of Special Education by Parents' Attorney

ATTORNEY FOR THE PARENTS: Could you please describe Matthew's typical daily schedule.

DIRECTOR OF SPECIAL EDUCATION: Matthew arrives at school by bus—

ATTORNEY: Regular or special education bus?

DIRECTOR OF SPECIAL EDUCATION: Special education bus, but it is yellow. He goes on his own to his locker to hang up his coat. He meets his teacher in her room. He occasionally participates in before-school activities with a self-contained class of children with communication disorders, seven children, all of average intelligence. He starts his day with his teacher, follows format of language development, math development, reading development, more or less the format of a regular school program, however, highly individualized. His specialists—speech, occupational therapist, etc.—work with him at given times during the day. He attends regular gym class, eats with the regular students, attends all assemblies. Some days he has field trips.

HEARING OFFICER: Please submit his schedule as evidence. Next question.

ATTORNEY: With respect to 504.3 of the regulations which require that School Committee submit to the Regional Review Board for revenue a child's placement prior to his being assigned outside the home school, that the school system must have a plan for providing a program within the district. Has such a plan been developed for Matthew?

DIRECTOR OF SPECIAL EDUCATION: To present to the state?

ATTORNEY: Yes.

DIRECTOR OF SPECIAL EDUCATION: No, it has not.

ATTORNEY: Is anyone at this point responsible for drawing up or preparing such a plan?

DIRECTOR OF SPECIAL EDUCATION: I would be responsible, and depending on the outcome of this hearing, if Matthew is ordered to an outside placement, I couldn't authorize that placement until I had approval from the Regional Review Board. I would have to state why it is I cannot provide a program in his own school system.

ATTORNEY: If you were ordered to provide a program inside his home school district, what would be your plans for this?

DIRECTOR OF SPECIAL EDUCATION: I would ditto what his Individual Educational Plan calls for now.

ATTORNEY: Matt's program provides for a great deal of mainstreaming, would you say?

DIRECTOR OF SPECIAL EDUCATION: Well, sure. We have to remember that his mainstream experiences increase as teachers get ready to receive him. Children are probably ready for this before teachers. Matthew's program calls for much individualized work in his academic subjects. But yes, there is opportunity for increased mainstreaming.

ATTORNEY: Are the nonacademic parts of Matthew's program important in his new education program?

DIRECTOR OF SPECIAL EDUCATION: I think they are very important. I am particularly interested in the development of Down's Syndrome children. I have worked with a number of them and I clinically note that when they are given social opportunities, rapid and steady growth can be realized.

ATTORNEY: I have no further questions for the witness.

HEARING OFFICER: Your next witness, please.

SCHOOL SYSTEM ATTORNEY: Please state your name, position and qualifications.

SCHOOL PSYCHOLOGIST: I am a school psychologist. I have an Associate's degree received in 1968. I received a Bachelor's in education in 1970 and a Master's degree in psychology in 1979. I had certification as elementary school teacher, and as school psychologist.

ATTORNEY: Do you know Matthew?

SCHOOL PSYCHOLOGIST: Yes, I do. I have seen him on a daily basis over the past year. I have also tested him.

ATTORNEY: You heard a description of Matthew, as in his Individual Educational Plan. Is this a fair assessment of Matthew's needs?

SCHOOL PSYCHOLOGIST: Yes, it is.

ATTORNEY: Do you have any other comments about Matthew?

SCHOOL PSYCHOLOGIST: It is difficult to make a statement about Matt's potential. However, Down's Syndrome children fall into a broad range of I.Q. from moderate to severe retardation.

ATTORNEY: Does this have any relevance to Matthew's program?

SCHOOL PSYCHOLOGIST: Yes. I think we need a teacher who has experience with severe special needs.

ATTORNEY: Would you agree that Matthew's social skills are a real strength of his?

SCHOOL PSYCHOLOGIST: Yes, they certainly are.

ATTORNEY: Does that have implications for his placement as well?

SCHOOL PSYCHOLOGIST: Yes, it does. It tells us that he has the potential to function within a community setting. He is able to make friends and will try and communicate with new people.

ATTORNEY: You made comments in three areas: program and community and vocational aspects. Could you comment further.

SCHOOL PSYCHOLOGIST: In regard to his program, Matthew needs to have other people to socialize with. He demonstrates potential here. In turn, he draws a great deal of popular response from others.

ATTORNEY: Do you think his present program is too restrictive in a social sense?

SCHOOL PSYCHOLOGIST: No, I don't. I think that many of his school friends can talk with Matthew through total communication.

HEARING OFFICER: Did you say teachers or students or both?

SCHOOL PSYCHOLOGIST: I was talking about both adults and students. Many of the students in the school really make an effort to spend time with Matthew.

ATTORNEY: Are you satisfied with the amount of mainstreaming Matthew is presently getting?

SCHOOL PSYCHOLOGIST: Yes, I am. My experience at his school is that the staff there is very willing to extend themselves for children who are handicapped.

ATTORNEY: Is Matthew able to tolerate a situation where he is the only student for a period or two of time?

SCHOOL PSYCHOLOGIST: Matthew has a very short attention span and it is very difficult for him to do some types of work other than in a one-to-one setting.

ATTORNEY: You also mentioned as important that certain aspects of his program should make it possible for him to function in the community. Could you expand upon those areas.

SCHOOL PSYCHOLOGIST: My understanding is that something new has happened to Matthew. That is, now he is able to use the telephone a little. He is able to call friends.

ATTORNEY: Were you a member of the team that visited some of the possible outside placements?

SCHOOL PSYCHOLOGIST: Yes. I visited all the possible placements.

ATTORNEY: I don't think we need to go into the programs felt to be inappropriate.

HEARING OFFICER: We have exhibits here on that.

ATTORNEY: Tell us what were the basic reasons for rejecting a program.

HEARING OFFICER: If it is different from what is in the record, OK.

ATTORNEY: Please just generalize for us.

SCHOOL PSYCHOLOGIST:

1. If the program did not have adequate opportunity for him to use sign language.
2. If the program did not have speech services.
3. If the program did not have A.D.L. skills.
4. Potential for occupational therapy and prevocational skills.
5. Good role models for Matthew.

ATTORNEY: What are good role models?

SCHOOL PSYCHOLOGIST: A chance for him to see other children who have age-appropriate behavior. Matthew models behavior very quickly.

ATTORNEY: What type of behavior would you not want him to model?

SCHOOL PSYCHOLOGIST: Self-stimulating behavior that might be seen if he were with autistic children; extremely acting-out behavior would be another example.

ATTORNEY: Any other elements that would make a program inappropriate in the programs you visited?

SCHOOL PSYCHOLOGIST: Community-based experience would be very important for Matthew.

ATTORNEY: What does this mean—going to shopping centers?

SCHOOL PSYCHOLOGIST: Yes, going to shopping centers.

ATTORNEY: Does this have to be in his home town?

SCHOOL PSYCHOLOGIST: If it were in other towns there would be less direct carryover into his own life. We try and make experiences as few steps away from concrete things as possible.

ATTORNEY: You had mentioned the importance of signing. How important is this?

SCHOOL PSYCHOLOGIST: I think it important for Matthew to have a wide variety of people to sign with. He needs to be able to sign with other adults, not just one other adult. He should be able to have children around him who at least recognize that he is signing, and perhaps can pick up on some of the signs that he uses.

ATTORNEY: Is it fair to say that the first five programs you visited did not comply with one or more of the needed elements for Matthew's program, and for that reason you found them inappropriate, not just less appropriate?

SCHOOL PSYCHOLOGIST: That is correct. I found the five inappropriate.

ATTORNEY: Did you visit the sixth program, which was a private school?

SCHOOL PSYCHOLOGIST: Yes, I did.

ATTORNEY: Could you give us your and possibly the team's reaction to that school—the types of children, teacher qualification and that sort of thing. Tell us when you visited and the length of the visit.

SCHOOL PSYCHOLOGIST: We visited the school on December 8, 1983, and stayed for most of the morning. Joining me were the speech pathologist, occupational therapist, and the learning disabilities teacher. Their private, nonprofit, 766-approved school has a student population of about 100 students. It is about 45 to 50 minutes from Matthew's home town.

ATTORNEY: Are there any other students attending from Matthew's home town?

SCHOOL PSYCHOLOGIST: To the best of my knowledge there are not.

ATTORNEY: Could you give us an idea as to the nature of the students' disabilities?

SCHOOL PSYCHOLOGIST: Yes. The students range in age between 3 and 22 years old. They are described as multi-handicapped.

HEARING OFFICER: I have a report written by the witness on this. I am taking it as her direct testimony.

ATTORNEY: I take it you made other observations that you did not write up. Look at what you have already written. Did you get a look at classrooms?

SCHOOL PSYCHOLOGIST: The classrooms were visually very attractive. The teachers were warm and pleasant. There was no sign language being used that I saw, nor did the rest of my team observe any signing with students.

ATTORNEY: How many classrooms did you visit?

SCHOOL PSYCHOLOGIST: We visited probably about 6 classes. Some were one-to-one teaching situations, some classes.

HEARING OFFICER: You said you saw no signing.

SCHOOL PSYCHOLOGIST: That is correct. I am told all the staff is trained to sign, and they would have that service available.

ATTORNEY: Did you see any of the students signing to each other?

SCHOOL PSYCHOLOGIST: No, I didn't.

ATTORNEY: Were you concerned about the lack of signing going on?

SCHOOL PSYCHOLOGIST: Yes. I am not sure of the amount of opportunity our student would have in that setting.

ATTORNEY: Did you have any other concerns about the students themselves?

SCHOOL PSYCHOLOGIST: All the students in the programs are very handicapped. No normal students attend the school. The program has a very strong behavior modification component to it, which seems geared to their severely behaviorally disordered children.

ATTORNEY: Would Matthew benefit from this type of behavioral modification program?

SCHOOL PSYCHOLOGIST: Matthew has behavior modification systems in place. However, he has progressed to a point where he is using social reinforcers, which is a far higher level than tangible reinforcers. It would be a step backward for him to be in a system where he would get these rewards.

ATTORNEY: Would it be possible to adapt the behavior modification program—did you ask that?

SCHOOL PSYCHOLOGIST: I observed that all the teachers wore aprons and handed out tokens.

ATTORNEY: What other observations did you make of the school?

SCHOOL PSYCHOLOGIST: It appeared that the staff was very involved with their students, interested in their students. Beyond that I don't know what else I can tell you.

ATTORNEY: Did the staff appear to be qualified?

SCHOOL PSYCHOLOGIST: We asked that question from the educational coordinator and did not receive a direct answer.

ATTORNEY: Did you think this school could meet the goals and objectives outlined in Matthew's Individual Educational Plan?

SCHOOL PSYCHOLOGIST: It meets a great many of the goals.

ATTORNEY: Which ones does it meet?

SCHOOL PSYCHOLOGIST: Occupational therapy, possibly the speech and language goals, the A.D.L. skills. I am concerned about the opportunities for good role models. I am concerned about the large number of behavioral problems, concerned about the lack of community-based experience.

ATTORNEY: There has been a stipulation that Matthew's program was appropriate for him. Would you agree—or disagree—that the program you saw last is similar to that program?

SCHOOL PSYCHOLOGIST: They have many components that are similar. However, the private school did not have as much mainstreaming.

ATTORNEY: Thank you.

Cross-Examination of School Psychologist by Parents' Attorney

PARENTS' ATTORNEY: Did you actually see the classroom that Matthew would be assigned to?

SCHOOL PSYCHOLOGIST: We actually don't know what classroom he would attend.

ATTORNEY: Could you explain why you did not know.

SCHOOL PSYCHOLOGIST: They told us they would like to see Matthew before they could assign him.

ATTORNEY: Based on the information you were able to give them, they could not make a placement.

SCHOOL PSYCHOLOGIST: They showed us classrooms and spaces that were very similar to those where Matthew would work.

ATTORNEY: How large were the groupings?

SCHOOL PSYCHOLOGIST: The groupings were small, individual at times. At times they were as many as ten, and when they had that many students, they had several other adults with them, depending on the type of activity they were engaged in.

ATTORNEY: Did you observe any classrooms in which total communication was offered?

SCHOOL PSYCHOLOGIST: I did not see any total communication going on.

ATTORNEY: Did you request to see classes where total communication was being utilized?

SCHOOL PSYCHOLOGIST: We told them at the beginning the type of classes we were interested in. We asked questions about who signed. We did not see anything going on.

ATTORNEY: Did you have any idea of how many children in the program required total communication?

SCHOOL PSYCHOLOGIST: I don't know.

ATTORNEY: Do you know if there are any?

SCHOOL PSYCHOLOGIST: They told us they do have some.

HEARING OFFICER: There would also be children, according to your testimony, who would also be on token economies as well as receiving total communication. Everybody seemed to be on a token economy?

SCHOOL PSYCHOLOGIST: Yes, it looked that way.

HEARING OFFICER: Thank you.

ATTORNEY: You stated in your direct testimony that good role models are important for Matthew. What exactly do you mean by a role model?

SCHOOL PSYCHOLOGIST: I mean someone whose behavior can be utilized as a positive example.

ATTORNEY: Is his current program a good role model experience?

SCHOOL PSYCHOLOGIST: Yes, it is.

ATTORNEY: You stated in your opinion the interim program by present staff would be an appropriate program for him.

SCHOOL PSYCHOLOGIST: Yes.

ATTORNEY: Would that also be an appropriate program as a long-term solution?

SCHOOL PSYCHOLOGIST: Yes.

ATTORNEY: Would a program that did not allow for Matthew to be mainstreamed be an appropriate program for him?

SCHOOL PSYCHOLOGIST: I would have real concerns about that because Matthew has such very good social skills. No, I don't think it would be.

ATTORNEY: I have no further questions.

End of cross-examination. Next witness called by the Hearing Officer.

ATTORNEY: Would you please state your name, your position and your qualifications.

WITNESS: I am an occupational therapist. I have been working as a therapist for 17 years. I have a Bachelor's degree from Tufts University, 1966. I have a Master's from Boston University in 1972. I have worked with developmentally delayed students both in the institutions and in the public schools. I am a registered Occupational Therapist.

ATTORNEY: Did you know sign language at all?

OCCUPATIONAL THERAPIST: I have what I would consider a moderate degree of signing. I have taken formal courses in signed English. I have two other students who are on total communication programs with whom I sign.

ATTORNEY: How long have you known Matthew?

OCCUPATIONAL THERAPIST: I met him in December of 1978.

ATTORNEY: Have you been working with him since then?

OCCUPATIONAL THERAPIST: I tested him first, then I have seen him once or twice a week.

ATTORNEY: Do you consult to the teachers as well as providing direct service to Matthew?

OCCUPATIONAL THERAPIST: Yes, on a weekly basis.

ATTORNEY: Would you say on a general basis that Matthew has made good progress?

OCCUPATIONAL THERAPIST: Better than good—excellent. When I first met Matt, he had a lot of behavior problems. Not acting out, but Matthew did what Matthew wanted to do, when he wanted to do it. However, there is very little behavioral difficulty with him any more.

ATTORNEY: Do you use any behavior modification systems with him?

OCCUPATIONAL THERAPIST: Positive reinforcement, in terms of praising him for a good job, bringing his bad jobs to his attention, telling him he could do it better and to try again. No tokens or food reinforcers or anything like that.

ATTORNEY: Could you tell us currently what Matthew would need in a program.

OCCUPATIONAL THERAPIST: In terms of my brand of occupational therapy, I am involved in fine motor and gross motor muscle development and the activities of daily living and occupational skill development. So far one of the key things in his program is maximizing Matthew's great aptitude to be a worker and a performer. We have started Matthew in a vocationally oriented component to his program two years ago—packaging and assembly, stapling and envelope stuffing. He was really good at this and could work for extended periods of time. At this point he can work for periods up to an hour.

ATTORNEY: Are there things that he can do around the school?

OCCUPATIONAL THERAPIST: Collating, sorting, business type machines, copy machines. Obviously as he is 10 years old he needs supervision. Very strong in work organization.

ATTORNEY: Would you say the opportunity to continue that type of activity would be an important part of his program?

OCCUPATIONAL THERAPIST: Yes, I think it is critical. Yes, in our thinking, that has been number one. More than with many children I have worked with, Down's Syndrome and otherwise. It's been critical for Matthew because this is a strength and we obviously want to teach to his strengths. Maybe one day Matthew could be in a nonsheltered type of an employable situation, because he is such a natural worker.

ATTORNEY: What other elements would you recommend to be a part of his program?

OCCUPATIONAL THERAPIST: I think he needs to continue work on motor development as a whole. Motor skills were not a strength for Matthew. He needs fine motor therapy that will enable him to be a competent and efficient signer—more fine motor jobs.

ATTORNEY: How is this carried out?

OCCUPATIONAL THERAPIST: He also attends a gym class with a communications delayed group which I run with the physical education teacher every week. You can really see how Matthew can interact in motor activities with children who are average cognitively but have some motor difficulties and language problems. He is equal to or better than some students in the class.

ATTORNEY: How does he get along with these children?

OCCUPATIONAL THERAPIST: He gets along fine—no problems. He needs no interpreter. There is a student in the class who signs. He is very much a part of the class, in a very appropriate way. There are children who are both older and younger in the group.

ATTORNEY: What about A.D.L. skills?

OCCUPATIONAL THERAPIST: They are parallel with vocational skills, and are really important. He learns very well from concrete situations. He can go out into his own community now and has been learning safety rules—crossing a street, going to a shopping center, the bank, seeking information, railroad crossing, seeing lights flashing.

ATTORNEY: How much direct service do you recommend by an occupational therapist?

OCCUPATIONAL THERAPIST: I would not want to get it down lower than two periods a week.

ATTORNEY: What would be the aggregate amount of time?

OCCUPATIONAL THERAPIST: An hour to an hour and a half.

ATTORNEY: Did you review the qualifications of his new teacher?

OCCUPATIONAL THERAPIST: Yes, I did, and I participated in the interview.

ATTORNEY: Do you consult to the current teachers?

OCCUPATIONAL THERAPIST: Yes.

ATTORNEY: Do you think the new teacher would be able to continue to work with you on a consultative basis?

OCCUPATIONAL THERAPIST: Yes, I do. I think also she is stronger in community skills—daily living and vocation skill because of her past work.

ATTORNEY: Did you visit any of the programs that have been described?

OCCUPATIONAL THERAPIST: I visited the most recently visited two programs.

ATTORNEY: Did you concur that the next to last program was inappropriate for Matthew?

OCCUPATIONAL THERAPIST: Yes.

ATTORNEY: Could you give us your impression of the last program visited?

OCCUPATIONAL THERAPIST: Strengths are that this has a strong vocational component, work activated, strong in activities of daily living, management of your own self. They have an occupational therapist who seems to be appropriately qualified. They have adaptive physical education. My main drawbacks are similar to the psychologist's. It is obviously a very behaviorally oriented program, a token economy, little aprons. I spotted that right away because I have worked in institutions. A lot have behavioral components. Many seemed cognitively average. That concerns me because social skills and behavior are really strong things for Matthew. I did not see total communication used as an ongoing casual part of things, in class or in the halls. That is important because it is a part of Matthew's casual day—used at lunch.

ATTORNEY: Was it in other respects conducive to his learning style, with the type of learning approach you would recommend?

OCCUPATIONAL THERAPIST: Yes, it was in the sense that they would praise him when he did a good job. I assume they would not be giving him tokens and M&M's. If that was not necessary. I would think they have a physical plant that would be adequate. Yes, functional skill approach—they do do community things when they are able. Day-to-day contact not there. Physical plant and a lot of the technical things are there.

ATTORNEY: Any other comments on this placement?

OCCUPATIONAL THERAPIST: One of my things—a personal kind of a thing. It is a very well ordered environment. To me, almost too much. Very structured. I felt a need to go back and rearrange my desk or something. More disturbed students could benefit—not Matthew.

Cross-Examination of Occupational Therapist by Parents' Attorney

ATTORNEY: Over the five years you have known Matthew, have you felt he has been making appropriate progress?

OCCUPATIONAL THERAPIST: Yes, and I think his communication has improved. When I first met Matt, you had a feeling he was saying something to you. There was the vocal inflection, but basically to me—and I work with a lot of severely handicapped and can understand a lot of poorly articulated speech—I could understand very little of what Matthew said, except "Ya." This must have been very frustrating for him. Now we are able to deal with him—to teach him a skill in a different way.

ATTORNEY: Tell me something. From your observations, do you feel in the last school observed, do you feel that all handicapped peers would be a better role model for Matthew as a developmentally stable youngster?

OCCUPATIONAL THERAPIST: I don't personally feel that way. I think Matthew has an uncanny ability to look about him, see what is going on around him, pick up what is appropriate in the environment and model. The whole environment at that school—students are not behaving appropriately. Matthew should be where most anybody knows how to behave, relative to their age.

ATTORNEY: Do you feel the interim program that has been described is appropriate?

OCCUPATIONAL THERAPIST: Yes, I do.

ATTORNEY: Do you feel that program would be appropriate for him as a long-term program?

OCCUPATIONAL THERAPIST: Yes, I do.

ATTORNEY: I have no further questions for the witness.

HEARING OFFICER TO SCHOOL'S ATTORNEY: Your next witness, please.

ATTORNEY: Would you state your name, occupation and qualification for the record, please.

WITNESS: I am a speech and language pathologist. I have 20 years of experience. Bachelor's degree, 1952—in English. In 1966 I obtained a Master's degree from Emerson College in speech and language pathology and courses to update my background in speech communications since then. Certified by American Speech and Language Association and certified as a Speech and Language teacher by the state.

ATTORNEY: You said you started working with Matthew in 1978, correct?

SPEECH PATHOLOGIST: Yes.

ATTORNEY: Did you work both on direct service and on a consultative basis?

SPEECH PATHOLOGIST: Yes, both diagnostically and program planning, and direct service for three summers. I have also been training all the people who work in his environment.

ATTORNEY: Would you agree that Matthew had made good progress in speech and language over the year?

SPEECH PATHOLOGIST: Yes, extremely exciting progress in the last couple of years. Now we can communicate well enough with him to share the excitement of the learning process. When his mind is clicking on something, we can follow the generalizations that he is making.

ATTORNEY: Why do you pinpoint it to two years ago?

SPEECH PATHOLOGIST: Because he started total communication then. He now has a vocabulary of over 600 words.

ATTORNEY: There has been reference made to the fact that Matthew has just recently had some ear operation. Do you have any comments on the impact of that from your perspective on his further development?

SPEECH PATHOLOGIST: Yes. He had tubes put in his ears three weeks or a month ago, and since that time he has been more completely articulating words, particularly of three syllables, and he is putting in short prepositions in phrases he had previously omitted, so that the "a" is in, the "to," the "for" that he used to skip.

ATTORNEY: Could you elaborate on or tell us what speech and language needs you see as being necessary if he is to interact in any program that would be provided for Matthew. What would be the goals, the essential pieces of his program?

SPEECH PATHOLOGIST: There are four areas that he needs help with in connection with his communicative abilities—direct speech, service about three times a week individually to include planning the programs. He needs to have aural rehabilitation. He has formed habits of listening to this information that comes in through his ears as well as he could. Supervision of teachers who work with him and peers with whom he associates—to assure development of the total communication skills in Matthew's living community. That includes parents and teacher, you see. I want a class established to teach sign language to others—children and adults.

ATTORNEY: How many people in his environment need to sign? You're not saying that all the children necessarily in the public or private school need to sign, are you?

SPEECH PATHOLOGIST: I guess the word "need" is the one I would stumble over. I think it would be desirable for as many people as possible in the environment to understand what he is saying when he signs, even if they don't all sign themselves. The bus driver, the janitors have all asked to have the signing vocabulary sent home. We now have a list of five or six people. I don't see limiting it.

ATTORNEY: What would be the third thing?

SPEECH PATHOLOGIST: Ah, the next thing is that he really needs an environment that provides good models for communicative interaction in terms of not only behavior but speech, total communication, and oral language expression at the complete sentence level.

ATTORNEY: So he needs models who are able to speak in full sentences, who are able to speak at all, and models who use total communication.

SPEECH PATHOLOGIST: Yes, models from play and work that interact with him personally in order to fulfill his needs, express feelings, and weigh information and experience.

ATTORNEY: So would there be only a sort of a spontaneous interaction or would there be a formal structure in modeling by a teacher or the speech pathologist herself?

SPEECH PATHOLOGIST: There are opportunities now for formal and informal speech. His present cooking class has a small group of four children, all who have needs that are fulfilled by this very carefully designed class. We go on a shopping trip and then they cook what we buy, but believe me, there are all kinds of math and language experiences that are built into that cooking experience. The fourth thing is an experientially based language program. He has a weekly trip to the community fire station, police station, restaurant, store, photomat, and post office. And then photographs are taken. So he comes back and he uses the photographs to relay the information and retell the experience and share it with whoever will listen.

ATTORNEY: You were part of the team that visited some of the outside placements.

SPEECH PATHOLOGIST: Yes.

ATTORNEY: Do you share the conclusion that five of them—the first five—are inappropriate for Matthew?

SPEECH PATHOLOGIST: Yes, I do.

ATTORNEY: Could you tell us what your impressions as a speech and language pathologist were of the last school.

SPEECH PATHOLOGIST: As a speech and language pathologist, I found it lacking in some aspects. It was a beautiful school and it was serene and very well organized. It had a lot of wonderful vocational opportunities. They have a model house in the building.

HEARING OFFICER TO THE WITNESS: Will you keep in your own area of expertise.

SPEECH PATHOLOGIST: I will—they did say that they had an in-service training program in total communication and it sounded as though the potential was there to develop that more extensively. At the current time I did not see any total communication interaction taking place. They also said that most of their programs are individual. They do not have self-contained classrooms, so you could not visit a classroom for an age group. Children traveled much as our high school students would. They would have a home room, but then for math they would go to one group. They would travel around.

ATTORNEY: But what is the relevance to the speech and language perspective?

SPEECH PATHOLOGIST: Well, it is hard to develop or interact communicatively if you don't have a group of people to do it with all the time. Every group is changing all the time, and they only have a very low number of children who use total communication and the children cannot talk or relate nonverbally. A lot of these children will be behaviorally in a very structured modification program and didn't seem to have eye contact.

ATTORNEY: Would you stick to speech and language area.

SPEECH PATHOLOGIST: That's communication.

ATTORNEY: I see. In other words, total communicative interaction you did not see.

SPEECH PATHOLOGIST: I did not see it happening there.

ATTORNEY: You mean on more than a verbal basis.

SPEECH PATHOLOGIST: Yes.

ATTORNEY: Is it your opinion that the interim program that has been described with his new teacher and continuing with the goals and objectives would be the appropriate program for Matthew?

SPEECH PATHOLOGIST: Yes, I do, and I feel that it can be improved. His present plan is due to be revised in February and he has really outgrown it. We are already working on other goals.

ATTORNEY: Do you feel his new teacher could carry out the program?

SPEECH PATHOLOGIST: Yes, I was unable to interview her but I would expect from what everybody else has said that she would be able to do this job.

ATTORNEY: Did it appear that the personnel at the last school visited would be able to carry out the direct service component of the program that you have recommended?

SPEECH PATHOLOGIST: Yes. They seem to have a very good speech therapy program. I didn't see any total communication being taught.

ATTORNEY: You were satisfied with the qualifications.

SPEECH PATHOLOGIST: Yes.

ATTORNEY: I have no further questions for the witness.

Cross-Examination of Speech Pathologist by Parents' Attorney

ATTORNEY TO SPEECH PATHOLOGIST: Were the programs proposed as an interim program to be continued as a long-term program with a new plan being developed—would you feel that would be an appropriate education program for Matthew?

SPEECH PATHOLOGIST: Yes, I would.

ATTORNEY: Does Matthew require more services than could be provided, more services than a 502.4 prototype—do you know of any services he is not now being provided?

SPEECH PATHOLOGIST: No. I would see us working toward a less restrictive program than what he has now. He would continue to need the tutorials he now has in the academic areas but more and more other school life activities.

ATTORNEY: I have no further questions for the witness.

HEARING OFFICER: Thank you. Who is calling Matthew's former teacher?

SCHOOL SYSTEM ATTORNEY: I don't know that we are calling her, do you? (The parents, lawyer, want to call her.)

ATTORNEY FOR PARENTS: Yes, I will call her.

ATTORNEY FOR PARENTS (calls Matthew's mother next): Witness (Matthew's mother).

HEARING OFFICER to Parents' lawyer: Do you want to make an opening statement? I just want to give you that option. You don't have to do it.

ATTORNEY FOR PARENTS: I will make a closing statement.

ATTORNEY to Matthew's mother: Why did you reject the educational plan?

MATTHEW'S MOTHER: We rejected the current educational plan because we didn't feel that Matthew was going to get the services that were written into the education plan that was supposedly meant to cover up to next February. He was getting a substitute teacher. We also did not feel that he had to go out of his own school system because we felt we had it. It was changed halfway through because the class which he was in was disbanded.

ATTORNEY: You have heard the testimony with respect to the interim program which will be implemented for Matthew with his newly hired teacher, the individual specialists who have been working with him these past years and the consultant. Do you feel that program is adequate and appropriate to meet Matthew's needs?

MATTHEW'S MOTHER: I do.

ATTORNEY: Do you feel that would be an appropriate program for more than an interim period?

MATTHEW'S MOTHER: I do, yes.

ATTORNEY: And why is that?

MATTHEW'S MOTHER: Because I think all these people are (I don't know about his new teacher because I haven't met her)— I believe and trust the judgment of all who have been working with him. They are very highly qualified and they know an awful lot more than I do as far as his development. I can't say enough. I think he is being offered perfectly suitable services and there is no need for him to go out of the district.

ATTORNEY: Do you feel that there would be any benefit for Matthew to be placed in a program such as the last outside placement visited with as many as 100 other special needs youngsters?

MATTHEW'S MOTHER: Not really, because I think that he does an awful lot of copying his peers. The more normal the situation can be, the better.

ATTORNEY: Are you and Matthew happy with his present placement?

MATTHEW'S MOTHER: He is very happy as far as I can tell. The change-over this year has been a little bit disconcerting because he had such a super team of people with him. The change was difficult.

ATTORNEY: Having Matthew in his local school—does that carry over into after-school life?

MATTHEW'S MOTHER: Yes, it does as much as it can. He doesn't have buddies who come over and hang around. He will have more people if he is at the home school than going away to school, where it would become more limited again.

ATTORNEY: Is there anything you would like to say that you would like the Hearing Officer to know?

MATTHEW'S MOTHER: I think the Hearing Officer knows from our preconference that I am very keen for Matthew to stay in his home school. He has a really nice time there. He should not go out to something that does not offer any extra, that will not give anything extra. I think it has been summed up by the specialists here. I agree wholeheartedly that he has made huge progress.

ATTORNEY: I have no further questions.

Cross-Examination of Matthew's Mother by School Attorney

ATTORNEY: How many children does Matthew interact with in the community?

MATTHEW'S MOTHER: Ah, I am not sure. At times he has a special friend. Sometimes she comes over to visit.

ATTORNEY: Is she from town?

MATTHEW'S MOTHER: Yes, she is. There are some friends of his brother who he enjoys being with. He likes to think he can call them up.

HEARING OFFICER: How old is his brother?

MATTHEW'S MOTHER: His brother is eight.

HEARING OFFICER: His brother is in Matthew's school?

MATTHEW'S MOTHER: Yes. He plays with his brother a great deal after school. No other children specifically at the moment.

ATTORNEY: You are satisfied or have been satisfied with the services provided for Matthew in the past—is that right?

MATTHEW'S MOTHER: Right.

ATTORNEY: Have you had any objections to the program that has been devised for him this year, other than the fact that his teacher is a substitute teacher?

MATTHEW'S MOTHER: Not really, except that the physical part—not being given the choice of a regular classroom. I mean, he does have a room now which may or may not fill the purpose. I would like to think that he would have a classroom that was a bit more of a normal situation.

ATTORNEY: What is the room like?

MATTHEW'S MOTHER: It has no windows—that bothers me. I think the fact that we weren't informed terribly well at the beginning about the breakup of his previous class—it seemed there was a lot not being told to us. I didn't like that.

ATTORNEY: You were informed at some point in time that the class was breaking up.

MATTHEW'S MOTHER: Yes, I agree. It was during the summer that we were aware it had broken up.

ATTORNEY: Didn't you get any indication earlier?

MATTHEW'S MOTHER: Not anything very clear. Maybe I am very slow or I hadn't noticed or something, but it didn't seem that the main point that the class was breaking up. Maybe I am getting a bit muddled at this point.

ATTORNEY: Did you agree that the class was broken up?

MATTHEW'S MOTHER: Well, yes. I doubted that actually. The teacher was also a little "at sea," I believe, as to what was going to happen for the following school year.

ATTORNEY: The teacher was the one who conveyed that the class was broken up?

MATTHEW'S MOTHER: Yes, she made it the clearest, but I wasn't particularly aware of it until afterward.

ATTORNEY: That was in the summer.

MATTHEW'S MOTHER: Yes, sometime in July.

ATTORNEY: Thank you. I have no further questions for the witness.

HEARING OFFICER: You mentioned that I had knowledge of things from the prehearing conference. One problem is that the prehearing conference is not on the record, so I just want to ask you one or two questions about that. Do you have knowledge of children from other towns who are interested in your son's program?

MATTHEW'S MOTHER: Yes. I believe at this point that the classmates he did have last year—that there will be the possibility of someone with similar special needs. I know that one classmate has just moved into the community in the last few weeks.

HEARING OFFICER: This student was in your son's previous program?

MATTHEW'S MOTHER: Yes.

HEARING OFFICER: Where did he go this year—do you know?

MATTHEW'S MOTHER: Yes. He went to a program in a neighboring town.

HEARING OFFICER: OK—thank you.

ATTORNEY FOR PARENTS: Just one last question. Did that student last year reside in your home town?

MATTHEW'S MOTHER: No.

ATTORNEY: I have no further questions for the witness.

Parents' Attorney calls the last witness—Matthew's last year's teacher.

ATTORNEY: Please state your name and background qualifications.

WITNESS: I have a Bachelor of Arts degree from the University of Maine in psychology, a Master's Degree from Lesley College as a teacher of special needs. Guest lecturer at Northeastern University, diagnostic work with deaf/blind students, and taught total communication to nonverbal students.

HEARING OFFICER: Are you part of the special needs collaborative where you are?

TEACHER: Yes.

HEARING OFFICER: Are you teaching a class or teaching teachers?

TEACHER: I am teaching a class.

ATTORNEY (for parents): In addition to your responsibilities as a classroom teacher, do you also hold the position as a consultant?

TEACHER: Last year in an adjoining town—this year I have been consultant to Matthew's program.

ATTORNEY: What do your duties involve?

TEACHER: Primarily working with his substitute teacher and doing teacher training with her in terms of developing curriculum. I outline specific skills that need to be addressed and help her to develop a teacher strategy for teaching those skills to Matthew—in addition, meeting with the other specialists on the team in an educational capacity to draw together an educational plan.

ATTORNEY: In addition to your role as a consultant, have you had any other involvement with Matthew?

TEACHER: He has called me on the phone once to invite me to his birthday party. Seeing him once after that was the extent of it.

ATTORNEY: And last year what was your involvement?

TEACHER: Last year I was his primary teacher.

ATTORNEY: And you were the person who was primarily responsible for providing service during the 1982–83 school year?

TEACHER: Yes, and I wrote the educational objectives for his Education Plan.

ATTORNEY: You have heard the testimony today with respect to the program. Is it your opinion that that interim program would be appropriate for Matthew?

TEACHER: Yes.

ATTORNEY: Would that program be appropriate if it were to continue as a long-term program?

TEACHER: Yes, it would. I would amend it by saying that I would like to see some more integration into regular classes.

ATTORNEY: And why do you feel that more integration into regular classes would be appropriate for Matthew?

TEACHER: As has been stated previously to this, Matthew learns best by modeling and having appropriate role models, and seeing consistent role models. Last year he had a classmate who was a Down's Syndrome child functioning at a higher level, and he strove to be like her. And, in addition, we had regular education students who came into the classroom to play with the class and to provide appropriate speech and language models.

ATTORNEY: Have you had any contact with the last school visited by the team?

TEACHER: No, I haven't.

ATTORNEY: Do you have any knowledge of that program other than what you heard today?

TEACHER: I have some of the program I previously taught in. We did consider students for that program and we did have several students come from that program when it was under a different name. Mostly my knowledge is from reading the brochure.

ATTORNEY: Most of the students that came from there to your program, were their handicapping conditions comparable to Matthew's?

TEACHER: No, they were much more severe. For the most part they were behaviorally disordered, severely emotionally disturbed, autistic-like, aggressive, self-abusive. One student had severe physical problems, which of course Matthew does not have.

ATTORNEY: You have heard the testimony with respect to the team's observation at the last school visited that they failed to observe total communication. Do you have any feeling as to whether such an environment would be appropriate for Matthew?

TEACHER: I don't feel it would be appropriate for him. In the classroom last year I found, because I was able to maintain total communication with him throughout the entire day, he picked up a lot more sign that if it was more structured. Last year's class was a language-based program, language going on consistently, verbal and signing. He saw regular education students having to conform to discipline in the halls and lunchroom.

ATTORNEY: Last year Matthew had the opportunity to be part of a special needs classroom and to be mainstreamed. This year it is my understanding that he is the only student in his particular program. Given that he does not have handicapped peers in his classroom, do you think another program that would provide him this would be appropriate?

TEACHER: No, I don't. Special needs individuals only make up 1% of the general population. You're tilting that balance if he is placed in a school with all handicapped. In real life that is not the case. Matthew is going to come in contact with many more "normal" people. It is important for him to learn to interact with the normal population.

ATTORNEY: The speech pathologist testified that rather than see Matthew move toward a more restrictive placement or prototype, she would like to see him move toward a more mainstreamed program. Based on your experience as his teacher last year and his consultant this year, do you think that's a realistic objective?

TEACHER: I think that it is realistic. It's going to have to be done in steps. He could not go into a regular first grade next year, not even with a tutorial, but he needs to have the opportunity to interact with nonhandicapped peers and then should be in structured as well as informal situations.

HEARING OFFICER: You said he needs additional mainstreaming. Where would you recommend it? In what classes?

TEACHER: At this point, art, music, gym, any and all school activities. Last year we did participate in the Christmas concert, recess, lunchroom, any type of after-school program. He is participating in the equestrian program which, granted, is a handicapped group rather than something the entire school participates in. Those skills are something that a lot of kids in his home town have—many have horses. He can interact with kids who would be jealous.

ATTORNEY: I have no further questions for the witness.

Cross-Examination of Last Year's Teacher by School Attorney

ATTORNEY: Do you agree with the statement of some of the team members that your program as it currently exists is inappropriate for Matthew?

TEACHER: Yes, I do.

ATTORNEY: Why is that?

TEACHER: The program which I am teaching this year consists of four students of varying skill levels. The one nonverbal student whom I have is totally nonverbal in that she has no communication skills whatsoever, no receptive or expressive language. The other three—one is the multi-handicapped student who was in Matthew's program last year, and again, he was accepted on a diagnostic basis because of the lack of another program. Last year, the same. He had just moved into the area and was in desperate need of a program.

ATTORNEY: Is this child currently appropriate for your classroom?

TEACHER: He currently is. However, his needs are very different from Matthew's.

ATTORNEY: But he was in Matthew's program last year.

TEACHER: Last year's program consisted, prior to his admission, of two students, so it was an extremely individualized program and in addition, I had the time to work with the two students prior to his admission in April. These two students became increasingly independent. They could move about the school independently. If we had not reached that level, it would have been much more difficult.

ATTORNEY: At the conclusion of the diagnostic period in your program are you going to recommend that he remain with you?

Would he be an appropriate person to be educated with Matthew currently?

TEACHER: Depending on the qualification of the teacher and the expectation of the program, it could go either way. He does not have the vocational skills which Matthew has. He has verbal speech which is intelligible, which Matthew's is not, but he does not have the physical capacity to sign to Matthew. The student is a spastic diaplagic hemiphegic, so has very little motor control.

ATTORNEY: Was he a negative influence on Matthew last year?

TEACHER: No, he was not. He was a positive influence on Matthew in that Matthew had increased responsibilities for doing things for him. He would get his walker, get his helmet, help him get onto his walker.

ATTORNEY: What about other students in your program—are they also inappropriate models for Matthew?

TEACHER: Yes, one student is four years old. The other student is autistic. They have autistic-like behavior. They are withdrawn. Speech is verbal, but is very perseverative. Cognitive level is much lower, so it is a very different type of program.

ATTORNEY: The fact that no one saw signing at the last school observed by the team does not mean necessarily that a teacher could not sign with Matthew even in a class—is that correct?

TEACHER: It would mean that the teachers would have to change their teaching style to include signing on an automatic basis.

ATTORNEY: Is that difficult to do—make that change?

TEACHER: It can be.

ATTORNEY: Does the interim program sound like your last year's program?

TEACHER: Yes, it does.

ATTORNEY: I have no further questions for the witness.

HEARING OFFICER (to the two lawyers): Thank you. Am I correct that you will give your final argument orally?

BOTH LAWYERS: Yes.

HEARING OFFICER: Do you have any further witness?

ATTORNEY FOR PARENTS: No.

HEARING OFFICER: Would you like to proceed with your closing statement.

Closing Statement of Attorney for Parents

Many of the people here have been at many other hearings. Certainly one of the things that has struck me about this hearing is how pleasant it is, and how much effort everyone has put into developing the program for Matthew. I think many of us who have been kicking around 766 feel that lots of people have forgotten the role of 766 is to mainstream kids and to make sure that handicapped children are not isolated in programs which do not, in fact, represent real opportunities for growth and development. I think everyone has devoted a lot of effort in helping Matthew and that it's been with good effect. He is a child who enjoys school, enjoys his community, and he makes significant progress from year to year. I think that it would be a very risky thing to interrupt that progress or start moving him to a more restrictive setting with peers who we have no reason to believe would be more appropriate peers, against the wishes of his parents and against the studied opinion of the people who have worked with him for all of his school life. I think the issues before us are really quite simple. Does 766 require a school system to provide a program in the least restrictive setting which is adequate to meet a child's needs? This child has made progress year to year under educational plans calling for his placement in a program in his home school. Though the program may not be ideal in every circumstance, the program has proven to be adequate and appropriate in that he has made progress in his last year's program and continues to make progress in the program he has had this year, even to the extent that, and notwithstanding the fact that, the Individual Educational Plan does not expire until the end of February. There is a real need to rewrite and readjust goals that he has already accomplished.

HEARING OFFICER: Thank you.

Closing Statement of Attorney for School System

I would like to thank the parents for the kind words in their expressions of support and confidence in the opinions and judgments that they expressed that Matthew's support team have always demonstrated. I would just ask you to bear that in mind. The fact that the parents have always been happy with our programs, always had a high opinion of the qualifications of the people that you see here today, as well as the other people who have been involved in Matthew's program, and we just ask that you also listen to professional judgments that have been expressed and base your recommendations on them. Thank you.

HEARING OFFICER: Thank you very much. There are two things— first of all—I guess three things. I will make it an interim decision. The town has complied with the order of the prehearing conference. I would expect that would be implemented pending the outcome of this decision. The approval to hire the new teacher is in the Director of Special Education's testimony. I believe that is all, and I will do my best to get you a decision in twenty-five days.

The Decision

The decision made by the hearing officer twenty-five days later was in the favor of the parents and the team. The conclusions of the hearing officer's findings stated:

The evidence is overwhelming that with the inclusion of the recently hired teacher or a similarly qualified teacher, that Matthew's program at his home school is the least restrictive, adequate and appropriate to meet Matthew's special needs.

His last year's teacher, the school psychologist, the occupational psychologist and the Director of Special Education all give extensive testimony on how Matthew learns best by modeling, thrives on mainstreaming experiences in gym, art, cooking, music, and lunch and has positively influenced other children in the school to want to develop signing skills.

During the last few years in his home school program, Matthew has made "extremely exciting" progress in speech and language areas since the implementation of his total communication program, has attained pre-vocational skills (testimony of occupational therapist) and has functioned well in his mainstreamed classes (testimony of last year's teacher, school psychologist, occupational therapist, and his mother). I was convinced by his mother's testimony, the home school staff and the occupational therapist that Matthew learns best in a mainstreamed environment which would not be available at the out-of-district placement visited by the team and has flourished in particular by being in his home school district. I was convinced as well that socially and behaviorally, Matthew has made great progress and is appropriately placed in an environment where he has proved he can model positive behavior of "normal" peers (testimony of school psychologist and last year's teacher) rather than taking a step backwards if placed in a strict behavior modification program at this time.

Though it would certainly be preferable for Matthew to have group academic experiences, I was convinced by the testimony of the school psychologist, last year's teacher, speech pathologist, occupational therapist, Director of Special Education and Matthew's mother, that Matthew has ample opportunity for integration into the mainstream of the school, and that the school is willing to consider additional mainstreaming when it becomes appropriate (testimony of last year's teacher and Director of Special Education).

Finally, given the manner in which Matthew has been successfully integrated into the home school, the mandates of both Massachusetts General Law, Chapter 71.B, and 20 U.S.E. 1400, et seq. requires mainstreaming him in the least restrictive, adequate, and appropriate program, which has been shown to be at home school in his home town, pursuant to a revised educational plan which indicates the addition of an appropriate qualified teacher.[5]

Matthew's support team was very pleased with the outcome of the hearing—a strong professional team had withstood external pressures and found its position upheld by the law. A student of law or a teacher in training will note after an analysis of this transcript that very few points of law were used to argue this case. The concept of "least restrictive environment" as used by the parents' lawyer and again by the hearing officer in his decision was the most heavily stressed. This concept is defined by Massachusetts Public Law 766 regulations as a program that, to the maximum extent appropriate, allows a child to be educated with children who are not in need of special education, and of course the placement outside the home school in this case which most closely met Matt's needs was a school whose entire population was in fact in need of special education.

9

A Close Look at the Law

As one reads and then rereads the texts of our special-education laws, state and federal, and absorbs their basic intent, the regulations begin to make a great deal more sense. There are nine basic concepts that are developed in our current special-education laws, which aim to:

1. Ensure that all eligible handicapped students receive a free, appropriate public education
2. Provide a continuum of special-education and related services that will meet the needs of all handicapped students
3. Secure those medically related services which, in general, are diagnostic and/or therapeutic in nature
4. Provide for educational facilities and services that are comparable to educational facilities and services available to non-handicapped students
5. Educate the handicapped student to the maximum extent appropriate with nonhandicapped peers in the least restrictive setting
6. Ensure that special education is an integral component of the regular-education program
7. Ensure active, joint participation of parents and school personnel in the development of a student's individualized educational program
8. Individualize the application of techniques, procedures, instructional materials, and equipment designed to facilitate educational success
9. Ensure that due-process safeguards are established and implemented for all handicapped students and their parents

These nine concepts, if thoroughly understood and properly implemented in our schools, can make the world of difference for handicapped children. The appendix to this book contains the Public Law of the Commonwealth of Massachusetts Chapter 766, enacted in 1972.

Funding for Special Education

Funding for special education comes from three sources: federal, state, and local. The federal funding sources are Title I of the Elementary and Secondary Act as amended by Public Law 89-313 and Title 6, Part B of the Education for all Handicapped Children Act as amended by Public Law 94-142, the federal law enacted in 1975. Scholars will note only very few differences between the two since the federal Law was based on the Massachusetts law. Funds under Public Law 89-313 were provided to supplement special-education services to handicapped children enrolled in state-operated and state-supported programs. Those of us who provide school placements for children previously enrolled in such programs are eligible to receive funds. Schools must make application to their state divisions of special education, reporting on the number of qualifying children on their rolls. Dollar amounts from my school system fluctuated anywhere from seven hundred dollars to nine hundred dollars per student. We had between seven and ten students per year for whom we were able to claim funds. Funds under Public Law 94-142 were appropriated to assure to all handicapped children a free, appropriate public education and to help states in providing this education. Funds, the directive said, were to be used to serve children in need of special education, also to serve children who are not receiving services and to help children whose programs are inadequate.[1] These funds are administered by the state board of education based on the total number of documented eligible students not already qualifying under Public Law 89-313. In 1979, Public Law 94-142 mandated that states must provide a minimum of 75 percent of their total allocation to establish a statewide per-pupil entitlement for the direct use by local education agencies. The remaining 25 percent could be used by the state to provide direct or support services in a discretionary manner.

Ten years of service delivery in the Commonwealth of Massachusetts under Public Law 766 has seen a 400 percent increase in the funds expended for special education. In fiscal year 1973–74, the local funding level was $70 million, state funding $31 million, and federal funding $3 million, for a total of $104 million. Ten years later, local funding had risen to $240 million, state funding to $147 million, and federal funding to $27 million, for a grand total of $413 million. With these substantial increases in funds being committed to special education came an equally impressive growth in the number of children benefiting from special services. In 1974 the state had 90,000 children enrolled in special-needs programs, and nine years later the count had risen to 130,000. The cost of educating special-needs children, figured on an average per-pupil cost, rose from $2,000 in 1973 to $3,500 in 1983.[2]

After the first four years (1974–78) of special-education funding in Massachusetts under the first Dukakis administration, many were concerned about the ill feeling that had developed between regular and special educators. Those who were primarily responsible for regular students felt that they were deprived of funds because, they said, so much had been allocated for special-needs students. To some extent this was true. All school funds, in a sense, end up in the same money pot,[3] and cities and towns were having to pay increasingly large dollar amounts even to maintain a status quo. In 1973–74 the local share was 67 percent, the state 30 percent, and the federal 3 percent. The state share increased substantially between 1975 and 1978. We should realize, though, that the overall cost of special education may well have decreased if we factor in the saving brought about by the move to deinstitutionalize the three- to twenty-one-year-old population and the return from private schools. The actual figures show a reduction of approximately 2,000 handicapped children in Massachusetts institutions since 1974, with 500 (ages three to twenty-one) still institutionalized. Well over 2,000 special-needs students have returned to the public schools from private institutions from within the state, and the number of special-needs students placed in institutions outside the state has almost halved. If we consider that the average cost of institutionalizing a student for one year is $43,000 as reported by the Massachusetts Department of Mental Health, then we certainly can justify an increased per-pupil cost for special education in the schools of $1,500 over a ten-year period. According to a recent study prepared by the Government Relations Department of the Council for Exceptional Children, it has been proved that the earlier intervention occurs, the lower the cost of education and the greater the productivity of the student. A 1980 study by Wood calculated the cost of providing special-education services at various age levels to eighteen.[4] Here is what happened:

Intervention at birth	$37,273.00
Intervention at age two	37,600.00
Intervention at age six	48,816.00
Intervention at age six with no movement to regular-education classes	53,340.00

A 1972 study by Fredericks et al. found that 65 percent of the variance in gains made by two groups of severely handicapped students was attributed to the number of minutes of classroom instruction provided each day.[5]

A review of rehabilitation statistics recently pointed out that the lifetime earnings of mildly retarded adults is many times the cost of their education—almost 6.1, adjusted for percentage employed.[6]

A 1976 study by Braddock calculated that income taxes alone generated from the gainful employment of a visually impaired person could produce savings for the community of $167,144.[7]

A report by the GAO in 1980 estimated that with vocational training, 75 percent of physically disabled students and 90 percent of mentally retarded students are capable at a minimum of working in a sheltered environment.[8]

A 1980 study of children who participated in the Perry Pre-School Project showed a 50 percent reduction in the need for special-education services through the end of high school. Also, the study found that when schools invest about $3,000 per pupil for one year of preschool education, they immediately begin to recover their investment through savings in special-education services.[9]

In 1978 the Boverini–Collins bill became law.[10] Its purpose, as supported by the advocates of special education, was to put a halt to the growing competition between regular and special education. The fear was that the substantial programmatical gains that had been realized in special education were in danger of being lost, and these two intelligent lawmakers saw the danger and moved against it. The bill uses a new measure of fiscal ability (ability to pay for education) based on equalized valuation per capita rather than equalization valuation per pupil. Another major difference, as pointed out in the *Cherry Sheet Manual,* between the old and the new formula is that the new system is not a reimbursement formula but rather a current funding formula based on current year's enrollments.[11] In contrast to the old Chapter 70, the new aid is to be distributed directly to regional school districts as well as to cities and towns. The new formula calls for calculating local support percentage times the local valuation percentage times the sum of the weight of full-time equivalencies in the current fiscal year times statewide averages current operating expenditures per pupil in regular day programs in the previous fiscal year. The bill—the new Chapter 70—places special education in the same equalized formula as regular education and adds $178.5 million, which has led to level funding in 1983. With the passing of Proposition 2½ in Massachusetts in 1982, local school boards lost their autonomy. The educational programs, particularly in less affluent cities, had suffered serious teacher cutbacks as a result of this tax cap. Alarming numbers of teachers have been laid off, with special education frequently becoming the whipping boy in these locations. The ultimate effect of this legislation will not be known for some time to come.

The Need for Change

I am of two minds when contemplating the best way to bring about needed changes in our special-education laws. Should one advocate new legislation or seek the revision of regulations either through executive orders or State Department of Education regulation revision? When I consider how inexplicit the language of the law is in regard to the human services, I am inclined to call for a comprehensive law to govern the human services. A careful study of the special-education laws currently on the books reveals, on the other hand, a comprehensive set of laws that, in the case of Massachusetts, has served us well for ten years (1974–84), although these laws do need fresh interpretation in the form of regulation revisions.

I shall not attempt in this book to draft a new set of laws to govern the human services. I shall only say that when such an effort is undertaken, it should be kept in mind that the human services and the public schools share responsibilities for service delivery to our special-needs population, and thought should therefore be given to working out a way for both to work efficiently toward common goals.

I wish to make some suggestions for those areas where the laws currently in effect might be reinterpreted or revised so that the gains made to date in service delivery will not be lost and so that children can better be served. The Bill of Rights for our handicapped and learning-disabled population is, I think, as sound today as it was the day it was written. Children under the law have a right to a multidisciplinary diagnostic evaluation, an individualized educational plan, placement in the least restrictive educational environment, and impartial due process under an appeals procedure, all at no cost to the parents.

It is right and fair that the preambles to our current special-education laws point up that all too often our public schools have not adequately and appropriately provided for the needs of handicapped and learning-disabled children. Consider the fact that of the more than eight million handicapped children in the United States today, more than half did not, at the time the federal law was passed, receive appropriate educational services that would enable them to have full equality of opportunity. Moreover, one million of these handicapped children were excluded entirely from the public school system and thus deprived of the chance to go through the educational process with their peers. These compelling facts carry us swiftly to the conclusion that the law was needed.

After ten years of administering programs under comprehensive special-education laws, with a previous ten years of administering regular education without them, I can unequivocally state that with the comprehensive laws we have been able to move more rapidly toward realizing adequate and appropriate service delivery for our handicapped. We have been able to use the law to back up our requests for improved and additional staffing, to use just one example. This, however, does not mean to say that we have arrived at a point where we can sit back and feel the job is done. Far from it. We have certainly set the stage for change and in fact have made some major inroads toward implementing a relatively new, comprehensive special-educational law.

Compliance Monitoring

Some areas of regulation warrant reemphasis, if not revision. Compliance monitoring is one such area under the law We might look to our state regional offices and their role in this process. A revised system of assurances that a continuum of programs exist within the schools to serve its identified handicapped population is needed. All too often schools are left to their own devices when it comes to program development. After all, not all children are in separate programs. Granted, each has his or her own individual education plan, but these plans are carried out in classrooms, learning centers, speech and language areas, counselors' offices, and vocational centers. These programs within the total school complex need to be examined regularly to ensure that each setting has entrance and exit standards tied directly to the concept of least restrictive educational setting. I fear we may have begun to allow a segregated special-educational delivery system, often designed to function outside the regular classroom, to work against the all-important concept that education is best for most children in the least restricted environment. A one-to-one relationship with a counselor in an office located down the hall from the classroom may not be the best setting for helping a child who is having difficulty getting on with his or her peers. An alternative to this setting might well be a counseling situation where the student participated in a mixed group discussion on why cooperation is essential to the success of a canoe trip that is being planned. The law puts forward the concept of least restrictive educational environment; we need the machinery necessary to ensure that indeed we are practicing this concept as we plan our school programs for the handicapped.

In-Service Training

Our comprehensive law calls for in-service training for regular and special-needs teachers. Too frequently we find that our regular teachers are not receiving the training that has been called for and that is absolutely essential if we are to implement the law successfully. We seem to have looked to the special-educators in our schools to take on the responsibility for the indoctrination and training of regular educators in the whys and wherefores of special education. This has proved to be a mistake on two counts: (1) the special-educators have had their hands full with the implementing of the new laws, and (2) it is not sound pedagogy for one peer to assume the responsibility to instruct another when the clear implication is more work for the regular teachers. Our regulations need to be more explicit as to the role of regular educators in special education, and we need to evaluate the performance of regular educators in that role.

Mainstreaming

The job of mainstreaming special-needs students into regular programs as it relates to the concept of the least restrictive educational setting needs more attention. I have examined many goals in students' individual education plans and rarely found any statements contained in them that spell out just how this important process is to take place. We need to promulgate clearer regulations in the area of mainstreaming children and find ways to ensure that these goals, once included, are effectively carried out. The child-study teams established under the law to carry out this and other dimensions of the law need to be evaluated against specific criteria to include the team's knowledge of the law; its awareness of program and placement options available to it; and its knowledge and utilization of multidisciplinary assessment, related services, and due process. Regulations should spell out the role of state regional offices in monitoring these teams.

The Appeals Process

The appeals process, as utilized both by parents and schools, needs to be reevaluated. We have not taken full advantage of the art of mediation. We should be training our professionals in the techniques of successfully mediating cases so as to reduce the number of appeals cases.

Other Issues

Commissioners, placed in responsible positions by the law, should by regulation be directed to sample the knowledge accumulated by the schools through their experiences in a systematic and democratic fashion. The official organizations supported by the majority of special educators should have representation at appropriate levels when state committees meet to consider substantive special-education issues or regulation revisions. Such a procedure should again be clearly spelled out by the regulations.

There is no doubt now that the time has come for substantial revision of the organization and delivery of the human services. It is very important that, as this happens, responsible representation from the schools is sought so that appropriate linkages between the human services and the public schools can be clearly established.

We have found that the best-laid plans implemented for severely handicapped children on a nine-month school-year basis, when services are needed for all twelve months of the year, are not effective for children. We must reexamine our resources and cooperatively work out ways to pool them so that children needing twelve-month programs get them guaranteed under the law.

The law addresses the withholding of funds from states if the letter of the law is not followed. It is, however, too quiet on the subject of mandated programs requiring guaranteed funding. There are those who argue that a mandated special-education program without guaranteed funding is not a mandated program at all. We have, I think, developed a very strong case for special education. We have demonstrated that education in the least restrictive setting—namely the public schools—can work best for many more children than we would have previously believed possible and that as we get better at this work, program efficiencies can bring about cost savings. So let it be said loud and clear across the land: *special education for handicapped and learning-disabled students deserves financial support guaranteed under the law.*

We have made tremendous strides toward successfully implementing our special-education law in our country. It is true that some states are further ahead than others. We must find ways to share our knowledge and our experiences so that each can benefit from the other's unique knowledge of how we can best implement our sound and comprehensive special-education laws. We must resist the temptation to criticize the law when puzzled by a complex problem or frustrated by a seemingly insurmountable structural barrier. The law is the message and we are the messengers. We must look to ourselves and be sure that we ask the right questions and seek the needed help, so that the language of the law can become a reality that is a true benefit to the children placed with trust in our charge.

10
What Does the Future Hold?

This book has told how important it was in the early 1970s to recognize the need for special education to establish itself on an equal and separate footing from regular education. The roles of special-educators had to be clearly defined, and the administrators of special education needed line authority equal to or above that of building principals. All this was in order to ensure that special education could become firmly rooted in regular schools on its own terms. It has been said that any towns or cities in Massachusetts whose leadership did not recognize these facts would run into trouble both financially and in implementing the special-education mandate given us through Public Law 766.

Every state now faces the challenge that Massachusetts faced over thirteen years ago, for each must now implement a program that guarantees free public education to their handicapped and learning-disabled population, and they must do this in the least restrictive setting, which of course for most students means the regular public schools. The contents of this book will, I hope, be useful to those who are either launching their programs or to those who have run into seemingly immovable obstacles that have prevented them from accomplishing their goals.

This concluding chapter may be looked upon as a blueprint for the future of special education. Offered here is a statement on each of the critical areas that I regard as being of fundamental importance for the next ten years of public special education. They are taken up in the following order: administrative direction, teaching team arrangements, master special-education team, the role of special-education administrators, the Bureau of Special Education Appeals, and the human services.

Administrative Direction

Superintendents of schools, principals, and special-education administrators should team together to develop a master plan for an in-service program involving all teachers, regular and special. This plan should be presented to the school committee for adoption as a top-priority goal. The in-service plan should be developed around the concept that regular teachers should learn that unique body of knowledge that special-educators have acquired and that special-educators should become familiar with the unique problems facing regular classroom teachers. The regular teachers would be learning assessment techniques, methods of developing teacher strategies, the intricacies of Public Law 94-142, how to write individual education plans, behavior management, and techniques of cooperative supervision. The special-educators should spend time in regular classes teaching students and so learning what it is like to teach a class of twenty-five to thirty students. They would learn how to set up a regular curriculum and to develop daily lesson plans.

Teaching Team Arrangements

After such an in-service effort has been successfully carried out, teams of regular and special teachers could be formed and assigned to clusters of regular classrooms. The success of this single in-service goal would substantially change the face of regular and special education. It would offer the opportunity to integrate more special-needs students into regular classrooms, and at the same time all students would benefit from strong teaching teams that would address the whole child's emotional, social, and academic growth.

The learning-disability centers as we know them today would be decentralized, and the teachers and aides would be assigned to teaching teams within the regular school. They could serve on several such teams in the building, concentrating on those teacher clusters that had the larger number of special-needs students. These changes would make for a less fractured student day and a less restricted total program. All individual educational plans would be jointly developed by these new teaching teams.

Master Special-Education Teams

Each school system and its area human service providers would jointly support master teams for every 1,500 to 2,000 students, made up of a school psychologist, speech pathologist, learning-disability specialist, occupational and physical therapy specialist, psychiatrist, social worker, and human service professionals. This multidisciplinary team would do all the assessment work for severely handicapped students. They would do the assessment work also for any students placed in programs outside the schools. The team would serve on a consultant basis to the newly formed integrated teaching teams. This innovation could only take place if the previously described in-service program had been carried out and the human service agencies made staff available to work on the teams.

The Role of Special-Education Administrators

Administrators of special education should have regular teaching experience, should be certified in one or more special education area, and should have knowledge of regular and special curriculum and a firm mastery of group dynamics and team teaching. These administrators would team with the principals to evaluate personnel and the programs being carried out by the teaching teams. They would be themselves directly responsible for the master special-education team's work in and outside the public schools.

The Bureau of Special Education Appeals

The Administrators of Special Education, a Massachusetts professional organization, has organized several regional groups across the state. Each region has the opportunity to write position papers on topics of interest or concern. Then they may seek the support of their membership and submit these papers to the full body of the state organization of special educators. Two groups have made efforts along these lines in the related areas of mediation and the appeals process. Reproduced below is the position paper on the appeals process voted on by the North East Region in Massachusetts on February 15, 1982, as the direction that it feels should be taken in the future.[1] Such revision in the law is seen as absolutely necessary, for, as stated previously, over half the cases now heard by appeals officers are decided against the spirit of the law—namely, that handicapped and learning-disabled students are entitled to free and public education in the least restrictive setting. The appeals office as it is now functioning is awarding decisions to private institutions guaranteeing them placements at the expense of the public schools. They should be seeing to it that programs are put in place in the public schools that will meet the needs of the students. The position paper that follows would prevent these unconscionable decisions and bring us back on target.

THE IMPACT OF DUE PROCESS ON SPECIAL
EDUCATION IN MASSACHUSETTS, FROM THE
PERSPECTIVE OF PUBLIC SCHOOL PRACTITIONERS

A. Background

Chapter 766 and P.L. 94-142 are the results of the historical view that particular groups of students were being denied their entitlements to a "free and appropriate public school education." The development of the Massachusetts Special Education Law and Regulations—Chapter 766—reflects a set of procedures designed to ensure that special needs students were to be included to the maximum extent possible within the mainstream of public school education. The concept of "least restrictive prototype" supports that stance. Theoretically, a student is viewed as normal until a thorough assessment procedure, conducted within a variety of procedural safeguards, has identified the student as having "special needs." The access of the parent to an elaborate due-process system further ensures the rights of the student. The concept of "least restrictive prototype" combined with highly specific due-process safeguards was based on the view that various groups of students were being systematically denied access into public school. There was, in addition, widespread criticism and litigation focused upon the methods and procedures utilized to identify and assess students. These methods and procedures were viewed as being responsible for the various forms of segregated placement that had little or no education and/or social benefits for students.

The Chapter 766 appeals process was devised as a mechanism that would support the inclusion of various groups of students into the mainstream of public school education. Most observers felt that the implementation of Chapter 766 in September, 1974 would signify the beginning of an enlightened social policy for previously disenfranchised populations of students.

1. Public schools would develop programs and services that would enable them to work with students that were previously tuitioned out under the state financial tuition provisions of Chapter 750.[2]
2. Legal and social pressures on State Mental Facilities to deinstitutionalize would be accelerated through the development of public school and/or collaborative programs capable of serving low incidence populations. More importantly, the pressure to institutionalize students would be decreased by the availability of collaborative programs which, when combined with alternative community-based residences, would dramatically broaden the scope of normalization opportunities.
3. The need for private day and residential schools would continue, but they would shift their focus to a more severely handicapped population. The total population of students served in the private sector would begin to decrease over time.
4. It was also argued that the financial costs for educating severely handicapped students would also be decreased while affording previously neglected populations of students a better educational opportunity.

Clearly the architects of Chapter 766 and P.L. 94-142 had reason to consider 1974 as the beginning of an enlightened social policy that would be responsive to the educational and civil rights of students with severe needs. The Appeals Process, it was envisioned, would prevent what heretofore was an exclusionary policy while vigorously supporting the principle of "least restrictive prototype." The influences of educational researchers, social critics, and the judicial system vigorously endorsed Chapter 766 as a soundly based statement that would advance the interests of students who were historically denied a public school education.

The discussion that follows will offer an interpretation of the Massachusetts experience as it relates to the Appeals Process. The primary source of data will be the generalized observations of many based on current experience as special education administrators in medium to large sized suburban school systems. Any assertions, interpretations, and conclusions in this statement reflect the collective viewpoint.

B. A Flight from the Public Sector

1. *Nature of Disputes* The majority of the disputes involving parents and public schools have centered around efforts of parents to obtain private placements outside the public school sector. The primary diagnosis has been "learning disabilities." Direct experience indicates that approximately 50% to 60% of the hearings have involved disputes focusing on public versus private placements involving students who are described as "learning disabled." There appear to be many fewer disputes involving schools recommending a day or residential placement while the parents are attempting to secure a placement within a public school setting, which is in direct opposition to what the architects of Chapter 766 thought would occur. Most appeals have focused on efforts by parents to have students removed from the public school setting. Critical analysts predicted that parents would focus on making programs and services more responsive to need *within* the public sector for various individual students and groups of students. From 1974 to the present time, the trend to remove students from the public schools has not changed. The principles of "due process" and "least restrictive prototype" in a majority of cases have become mutually exclusive concepts rather than complementary and closely intertwined philosophical tenets. Interestingly enough,

there have been relatively few hearings that have involved severely, developmentally disabled students attempting to secure services outside of the public sector. The parents of those students have historically devoted their energies to the aim of public school inclusion and the development of better programs and services within public schools. It appears that the Appeals Process has suited the needs of that population of parents and students extremely well. The focus has been on developing responsive and comprehensive programming within public schools rather than a thrust to tuition students into day or residential settings.

2. *Procedural Flaws and Weaknesses* The Massachusetts experience in the Special Education Appeals Process is unique. From 1974 there has been a relatively sophisticated appeals system in place. One significant flaw with the process has been that any complaint or concern that propels a parent to reject an IEP [individual education plan] can trigger a complex administrative response involving the public school, the state, legal representatives, outside expert witnesses, private evaluators, and others in a hearing. Chapter 766 regulations do not provide any mechanism that would prohibit the extent of recourse in relationship to the severity of the child's problem. At worst, the appeals procedure supports the exploration and potential finding of a day or residential placement that may have little or no relationship to the extent of a child's special needs. Of further importance may be the fact that the present structure of the Appeals Process may increase and/or produce a state of alienation between the parents and the school. It should be understood that parents very naturally want to obtain for their children what they believe is the best in educational services. Parental aspirations, however, may not currently reflect those assumptions manifested by educational and social observers that provided the stimulus prior to 1974 for the creation of Chapter 766. Today, the Appeals Process, once initiated, can consider an entire universe of options. These options may include relatively expensive day and/or residential placements for every student who becomes the subject of a hearing regardless of the possible inappropriateness of such a placement and with total lack of consideration of existing local facilities. It seems that a major goal for most parents who elect to go to a hearing is the securing of a private day

or residential placement rather than a program within the public schools.

3. *Quality and Direction of Decisions* The most current revisions of Chapter 766 regulations made more visible the emphasis on least restrictive prototype. While the appeals process in Massachusetts provides individualized justice for specific students, it has not substantially directed its decisions toward increasing the capacity of the public schools to be more inclusive. It is our conviction that the focus of the Appeals Process has been directed at the "wrong issues." The major thrust has been on cases which compare public versus private placements for a population of mild to moderately handicapped students described as "learning disabled." The issue that arises is twofold:

a) How can schools move toward serving more severely handicapped students within the public sector, and
b) How can the Appeals Process become a more effective agent in helping schools become more inclusive?

C. Areas to Explore

For historical, legal, and philosophical reasons, public schools must continue to meet the requirements of a due-process procedure. That requirement should be viewed in optimistic terms. The Appeals Process (as a functional aspect of Chapter 766) should be structured in such a fashion that the overwhelming percentage of findings would have a direct and indirect effect on increasing the inclusiveness of programs and services within the public sector. The following are areas suggested for exploration and/or action:

1. The Bureau of Special Education Appeals must introduce a mechanism that addresses the question of creating a limited range of alternatives that a hearing officer might ultimately consider at a hearing. Simply stated: For those students with mild to moderate special needs, the recourse that a parent may obtain at a hearing should be limited as a function of the process. Prior to a hearing, a third party(s) or a panel of mediators would evaluate the evidence (Core Evaluation Team material, independent evaluation, etc.). The basic answers that may be forthcoming include the following:

a) "Yes—this case can go forward and the hearing officer can consider the possible recourse of a day or residential placement among the total universe of findings."

b) "Yes—this can go forward, but the hearing officer may not consider either a day or residential placement as a potential entitlement. The focus of the hearing will be on considering the Individual Educational Plan, hereafter referred to as IEP, in reference to the public school program setting."

c) "No—this case cannot go forward because there are no intrinsic merits to the case."

A significant number of cases could be quickly resolved without violation to due process. The focus of appeals hearings would shift to issues that focus primarily on the quality and responsiveness of public school programs. There would be a decreasing percentage of cases that focus on public versus private placement. It would seem that the premises of "least restrictive prototype" and "due process" would be reestablished as closely intertwined and complementary concepts that would maintain a continuing and positive influence on public schools. It would seem to follow that the person making that initial judgement would best be drawn from an impartial pool of individuals with background and training in special education.

Another version of mediator(s) involvement would be to strengthen the function of the role to the extent that the mediator(s) recommendations for resolving issues *must* be tried prior to the appeals hearing, e.g., a student would be assigned a three to six month period in a (502.3 or 502.4 Prototype)[3] setting in a public school before the final hearing as a good faith exercise in the spirit of the "least restrictive prototype" concept as put forth in Chapter 766 regulations.

2. Consideration should be given to introducing the "third party," independent expert approach. Very simply, the Department of Education should support the utilization of expert third parties who would perform the following activities:

a) Inspect assessment date (CET material, independent evaluations, IEP, etc.).
b) Observe the IEP placement and the student.
c) Take additional steps if required.

It is our conviction that a significant number of cases could be resolved quickly and inexpensively. The utilization of the "expert" approach could incorporate the observation of the parent alternative. The "expert" would respond to the following question. "Is the proposed IEP placement and program adequate and appropriate to meet the student's special needs?" If the "expert" responded positively that would conclude the process. If the "expert" indicated that the LEA placement was inappropriate he/she would observe the parent alternative. Based on that observation, the expert could either say, "Yes, the parent's alternative is adequate and appropriate," or, "No, the parent's alternative is inadequate and inappropriate." In the latter situation the dispute would then move forward to a hearing. Hopefully a procedure like this would lead to a speedy and equitable resolution for a substantial number of cases. The student's interests would be protected and would be supported while a more effective allocation of scarce financial resources would result. The basis of the decision would relate to educational rather than legal issues solely.

3. The Department of Education hearing officers have performed at a high level of competence considering the extraordinary pressure that is inherent in the hearing process. In 1974 the former Assistant Commissioner for Special Education indicated that it would probably not be advantageous to the interest of a school system to utilize a lawyer. At that time that appeared to be a discerning observation. Today, the complexion of a hearing has dramatically changed. It is not uncommon to participate in several days of hearings, utilize subpoenas, develop complex approaches, and engage in a variety of legally dominated strategies. The direct and indirect costs to parents, school budgets, and programs are staggering. There must be greater attention directed toward a restructuring of the Appeals Process that would decrease the number of hearings and change some of the characteristics of the actual hearing.

a) Much greater emphasis must be placed on supporting a speedy hearing process. It should be a rare and unusual hearing that would go beyond 2 days.
b) The range of alternatives which a hearing officer can consider should be narrowed and in many cases should decrease the amount of time that would be spent at a hearing.
c) Utilization of third party experts with special education training and background could resolve a significant portion of appeals cases quickly and in the interest of the student at a greatly reduced social and financial cost for all parties.
d) Technical and procedural eccentricities inherent in Chapter 766 [see Appendix] should be studied with a view toward making some needed changes.

D. Conclusion

There are many other areas that could be discussed. Comments have been directed toward those areas that are felt to be important to developing an understanding of the Massachusetts dilemma. The federal P.L. 94-142 and state (Chapter 766) laws and regulations were designed to support the inclusion of groups of students into the mainstream of the public school and the community to the maximum extent possible. That viewpoint was reflected in the notion of "least restrictive prototype" and an elaborate due-process mechanism that was designed to ensure that, to the maximum extent possible, students would be included in the public school settings. A substantial portion of the cases and decisions have reflected a different view than legislators, social critics, professionals, lawyers, parents, and others had anticipated. The philosophy that supported that initial perception was characterized by the following values:

1. We should involve all individuals in the most normalized environment possible.
2. We are more like than unlike others whom we have labelled with injurious and enduring effects in the past.
3. An individual should have access to family community, and all of the institutions that are available to all others in society—to the maximum extent possible.

Unless we are prepared to reject those values, then the legal and procedural mechanisms that have been developed to ensure the interests of students must speak more directly to supporting those beliefs. To summarize:

1. Under very specific conditions, certain cases should not be allowed to go forward.
2. Increased utilization of third parties to review evidence, observe the LEA program, and render a decision should be undertaken.
3. A careful monitoring of appeals should be instituted so that a speedy process is encouraged and becomes the standard.
4. The initiation of research that evaluates the hearing process, studies and disseminates case findings, and is more clearly identified with supporting change within public schools should be expedited.

Given the pressures on the Appeals Process, it has responded eminently well to the specific needs of individual children. That characteristic should be preserved while redirecting its focus to a more vigorous support of helping the public schools become increasingly responsive and inclusive as an institution. Social policy demands this type of orientation.

It is hoped that this statement will assist all parties including parents, public school practitioners, private schools, governmental bodies, and others in assessing the situation, and developing directions and approaches that will better serve the interest of special needs students. Finally, it is our conviction that unless a significant and thorough evaluation and redefinition of the approach to this problem occur now, we will have produced a system that has propelled a large number of students out of public schools and their local communities, toward a new policy of institutionalization. Combined with that policy, it is certain that in this era of shrinking fiscal and community support for expensive tuitions there will be a number of students who do require such placements who will not have access to those placements. We must manage scarce resources more effectively, restore public confidence, and match students, settings, and resources more competently than we have in the past eight years since the inception of Chapter 766.

Human Services

It is proposed that public education, the Department of Social Services, the Massachusetts Rehabilitation Commission, the Department of Mental Health, the Department of Public Health, the Massachusetts Commission for the Blind, and the juvenile court system along with the Department of Youth Services and the Office for Children each make the commitment to staff a master interdisciplinary team to serve each city and town in the Commonwealth. This team is to function as the assessors of special needs, case managers, and placement decision-makers for all ages of handicapped persons residing in its area. Much of the work now being done by agencies and departments will continue. The marked difference will be that any student or adult needing a combination of services will be jointly assessed by the teams. The special-needs population of each town and city will be identified, and all services will be available based on need. The individual and his or her family could receive medical care from the Department of Mental Health Regional Centers, family counseling from the Department of Social Services, vocational training and job placement from the Massachusetts Rehabilitation Commission, mobility training from the Commission for the Blind, dental care from the Department of Public Health, outward-bound-type training and legal service from the Department of Youth Services, and advocacy from the Office for Children.

If such a team became operational and continued to be involved through the entire period of need, no one would fall between the cracks that inevitably appear when agency competes with agency and education becomes the catchall for direct service delivery. Clients leaving Department of Mental Health facilities for community residences would continue to receive the needed care. They could return to the facilities for treatment, or the facility could reach out into the community. The great debate over whether we need state treatment facilities if we are committed to deinstitutionalizing patients would be put to rest, for a clear need for both would have been established. It is suggested that certain cities and towns be selected for the implementation of pilot projects, which would be evaluated after a year's operation. The following is a hypothetical case history as it might be written up in 1990. The case history of Michael Brown from Middletown, U.S.A., and was included in testimony I presented to the State Legislative Committee on Education at the State House, Boston.

Michael Brown, aged four years, arrived in Middletown, U.S.A., in January 1990. He had become a ward of the state, being the sole survivor of an airplane crash which had taken the lives of his entire family. He is diagnosed as a Down's syndrome child and as being moderately developmentally delayed. The joint Educational and Human Services team from Middletown was notified by the Executive Office of Human Services that Michael was to be placed in a foster home in that city. The team met, reviewed the child's background, and determined what additional assessment was needed. They developed a joint individualized education and treatment plan. The educational plan called for early-childhood placement in the public schools, including a readiness curriculum, occupational therapy, physical therapy, and speech therapy utilizing a total communication approach. The treatment plan called for family counseling with an emphasis on child management and behavior modification methods that could be used at home. Michael would return once a month to the Department of Mental Health's Regional Center for a physical examination. He takes medication for a heart condition, not uncommon in Down's syndrome children.

Michael progressed well through the years, his educational plan was modified by withdrawing his occupational and physical therapy treatment because his gross and fine motor skills had progressed to a point where the team felt there was no longer a need for therapy. By high school age, certain willful adolescent behaviors were manifest in his aggressiveness towards female peers. The team met to discuss this and modified his plan by changing the counseling goals. Michael eventually adjusted well to high school. Halfway through high school, Michael's prevocational teacher reported at the annual joint team meeting that Michael was showing an aptitude for carpentry. It was arranged that he and his foster father take an extra evening carpentry course at the local vocational school.

It took Michael until age twenty-two before he received a special diploma jointly granted by the school and the Executive Office of Human Services. The year leading up to his graduation had been a very busy one, for the Massachusetts Rehabilitation Commission had been eager to be involved and to work with the Department of Public Works' Division of Carpentry, to prepare them for Michael's arrival at his first real job after graduation. This city was now proud to state that it had developed 1,005 paid jobs for the handicapped. Michael's graduation day was dramatically moving. In attendance were the teachers, human services clinicians, and his future employer, with the commissioner from the Executive Office of Human Services awarding diplomas.

Of course, before dreams can become reality, a number of details would have to be worked out, such as offering incentives to cities and towns that showed a willingness to participate by establishing job locations for the handicapped. Jobs would have to be assigned to students one year in advance of building an individualized life plan so that both the employer and employee could be adequately prepared and job satisfaction and success ensured. It seems a logical progression that the individualized education and treatment plans should be followed by individualized life plans and that these plans would be monitored by joint education and human services teams for as long as support was needed. A new era of joint planning in a cooperative atmosphere could be achieved if such a plan were to be put in place, and it would then be hard to understand why we had tolerated those old days of frustration caused by a lack of cooperation between education and the human services.

Concluding Remarks

The opportunity to spend a year of study and work abroad proved a most stimulating experience for me. It set the stage for this book. I urge any administrator, whenever possible, after seven years at work, to seek a sabbatical experience.

The fact that the Commonwealth of Massachusetts enacted a special education law made my career in special education productive. I support that law and contend that without it we would not have been able to help as many of our handicapped children as we have.

Without the team concept which is tied to a multidisciplinary approach to problem solving and treatment plan development, we could not have sorted out the many challenges presented to us. The Massachusetts human services are to be given credit for demonstrating their willingness to support and fund a significant collaborative effort in service delivery.

Having a psychiatrist and attorney to work with was of the utmost importance for me. The severe handicaps of the children coming to the schools required a doctor's judgment and advice. The complex and intense involvement of the teams over contested placement required the objectivity of an attorney.

I am convinced that the best programs in special education can be built by becoming thoroughly familiar with the content of the special education law and creatively interpreting it as it relates to each individualized education or treatment plan.

I believe that if we are to hold the ground we have gained in special education, we professionals must work at becoming an integral part of the total school and the community it serves. The time has come not only for mainstreaming special education students but also for mainstreaming special educators.

What needed to be said has now been said, and it is sincerely hoped that this book will assist those who are responsible for making the laws, raising children, and teaching children to support and further develop our system for educating special-needs students. In its totality this book offers testimony to the dictum that there is no such thing as a disability, but rather there are only varying degrees of ability. If we make regular schools special, what was once only a dream can become a reality for all our nation's learning-disabled and handicapped children.

Appendix

When wrestling with issues around the implementation of our special education law, I have found that direct reference to the law is often far more helpful than mulling over the regulations that have been written around it. For this reason, it is included here. If, however, the reader wishes to refer to the regulations, they have been recently revised and may be obtained through the Secretary of State's Book Store, State House, Boston, Massachusetts 02133.

Chap. 766. AN ACT FURTHER REGULATING PROGRAMS FOR CHILDREN REQUIRING SPECIAL EDUCATION AND PROVIDING REIMBURSEMENT THEREFOR.

Be it enacted, etc., as follows:

SECTION 1. The General Court finds that past development of special education programs has resulted in a great variation of services to children with special needs with some children having a greater educational opportunity than others in less favored categories or environments. The General Court further finds that past methods of labeling and defining the needs of children have had a stigmatizing effect and have caused special education programs to be overly narrow and rigid, both in their content and their inclusion and exclusion policies.

In the light of the policy of the commonwealth to provide an adequate, publicly supported education to every child resident therein, it is the purpose of this act to provide for a flexible and uniform system of special education program opportunities for all children requiring special education; to provide a flexible and non-discriminatory system for identifying and evaluating the individual needs of children requiring special education; requiring evaluation of the needs of the child and adequacy of the special education program before placement and periodic evaluation of the benefit of the program to the child and the nature of the child's needs thereafter; and to prevent denials of equal educational opportunity on the basis of national origin, sex, economic status, race, religion, and physical or mental handicap in the provision of differential education services.

This act is designed to remedy past inadequacies and inequities by defining the needs of children requiring special education in a broad and flexible manner, leaving it to state agencies to provide more detailed definitions which recognize that such children have a variety of characteristics and needs, all of which must be considered if the educational potential of each child is to be realized; by providing the opportunity for a full range of special education programs for children requiring special education; by requiring that a program which holds out the promise of being special actually benefits children assigned thereto; and by replacing the present inadequate and anti-equalizing formula for distribution of state aid for special education programs with an equalizing one which encourages cities, towns and regional school districts to develop adequate special education programs within a reasonable period of time.

Recognizing that professional services and resources must be made available to cities, towns and regional school districts on a regional basis if this act is to be implemented successfully, and within a reasonable period of time, this act strengthens and regionalizes the division of special education in the department of education and provides for and urges meaningful cooperation among agencies concerned with children with special needs.

Recognizing, finally, that present inadequacies and inequities in the provision of special education services to children with special needs have resulted largely from a lack of significant parent and lay involvement in overseeing, evaluating and operating special education programs, this act is designed to build such involvement through the creation of regional and state advisory committees with significant powers and by specifying an accountable procedure for evaluating each child's special needs thoroughly before placement in a program and periodically thereafter.

SECTION 2.   Chapter 15 of the General Laws is hereby amended by adding after section 1L the following five sections:-

Section 1M.   The powers and duties of the division of special education, established by section one F, shall include the following: (1) to regulate, consult with and assist school committees in the identification, classification, referral and placement of children requiring special education; (2) to regulate all aspects of, and assist with, the development of all special education programs supported in whole or in part by the commonwealth; (3) to coordinate the expertise of professionals from appropriate disciplines, both within and outside of the department and to be the coordinating agency for all state agencies providing educational assessment services and educational services to children requiring special education; (4) to compile data on, and to require all public schools and agencies and any private schools or agencies receiving any funds from the commonwealth to provide information relating to, all children requiring special education who reside in the commonwealth and on all available special education programs supported in whole or in part by the commonwealth; (5) to periodically review and analyze said data in order to evaluate said programs and to disseminate statistical data to any citizen or agency within the commonwealth upon request; provided, however, that records pertaining to individuals shall be kept confidential; (6) to develop public information programs regarding the nature and extent of special educational needs of children residing in the commonwealth and the availability of special education programs to meet those needs; (7) to develop and recommend to the board of education certification standards for educational personnel employed in special education programs and regulations to encourage greater use of ancillary personnel; (8) to cooperate with and assist public and private colleges and universities within the commonwealth in developing courses and programs best designed to prepare graduates to serve the educational requirements of children requiring special education; (9) to receive and investigate complaints and to conduct public and executive hearings with power of subpoena on behalf of an individual child or group of children receiving or requiring special education regarding any aspect of any special educational programs and to initiate its own investigation without a complaint; (10) to receive and allocate federal and state funds for programs for children requiring special education, subject to the priorities established by this section and chapter seventy-one B and such other additional priorities as may be established pursuant to section one P by the board of education; (11) to recommend to the board of education such rules, regulations and guidelines and to issue such directives as are necessary to carry out the purposes of sections one N to one Q, inclusive, and to execute other provisions of law relative to the administration of educational programs for children requiring or receiving special education; (12) to provide for the maximum practicable involvement of parents of children in special education programs in the planning, development, and evaluation of special education programs in the districts serving their children; (13) to approve the purchase, lease and maintenance of all special equipment for the instruction outside of the classroom of handicapped children from whom attendance in public school is not feasible and to regulate the conditions under which such a child may be considered so handicapped; (14) to investigate into and hold hearings upon prima facie denials of equal educational opportunities by reason of national origin, sex, economic status, race, religion, or physical or mental handicap of school aged children requiring special education as defined in section one of said chapter seventy-one B and thereafter issue such declaratory and injunctive orders as may be necessary to cure any actual denials of equal educational opportunities by reason of national origin, sex, economic status, race, religion, and physical or mental handicap of school aged children requiring special education; (15) to require public or private schools and educational agencies receiving any funds from the commonwealth to establish cost accounting and reporting procedures, forms, schedules, rates and audits in conformity with department standards; and to make reports to the department at such times, in such fashion and on such forms as the department may require; (16) to conduct or contract with any federal, state or private agency for the conduct of research and development projects designed to improve the quality of special education programs or increase the efficiency of such programs; (17) in the event of funding shortages, to allocate resources proportionately; (18) to provide for placement of children requiring special education into public schools or agency programs near their place of residence and to allow other placements in the event that suitable public programs or services can not be provided; (19) to take all steps, including but not limited to public hearings and investigations necessary to insure that state and local expenditures for special education provide the maximum feasible benefit to every child receiving or requiring special education; (20) to develop and recommend any appropriate parent or guardian counseling or educational programs which are deemed necessary for the educational development of a child with special needs; (21) to recommend to the board that it withhold funds for special education programs from cities, towns or school districts, private schools or agencies which do not comply with regulations or statutes related to special education programs or do not carry out plans for such compliance within a reasonable period of time provided; however, that nothing contained in this clause shall be construed to prevent the board from withholding state and federal funds to the extent it deems necessary as provided in section one G.

Section 1N.   There shall be in the division of special education a sufficient number of bureaus to enable it to carry out its powers and duties under section one M, and the board of education, upon the recommendation of the commissioner of education and the associate commissioner for special education, shall appoint a director with experience in the education of children with special needs for each bureau. One bureau shall be responsible for holding hearings and conducting investigations pursuant to clauses (8), (13) and (18) of section one M, section one P and section three of chapter seventy-one B.

Section 10. There shall be established in each of the department of education regional offices a regional branch of the division of special education. Each regional branch shall be headed by a director with experience in the education of children with special needs and who shall be appointed by the board of education upon the recommendations of the commissioner of education and the associate commissioner for special education. Said regional branch shall have the following functions: (1) to consult with and assist school committees in implementing the regulations, guidelines and directives of the department in the area of special education; (2) to directly assist school committees in identifying, diagnosing and evaluating children with special needs and in developing special education programs to meet their individual educational needs; (3) to approve all special education placements by school committees of children with special needs; (4) to assist and encourage the formation of joint agreements between two or more school committees for the provision of special education pursuant to section four of chapter seventy-one B; (5) to investigate and evaluate any special education program at the request of the department or on its own initiative; (6) to maintain a list and inform school committees of professional personnel within and without the region qualified to assess children with special needs pursuant to the provisions of section three of said chapter seventy-one B and to make such information available upon request to parents, guardians or persons with custody of such children; (7) to have such other responsibilities as may be delegated to it by the department.

Section 1P. There shall be established in each region a special education advisory council, hereinafter called the advisory council, consisting of at least sixteen members, appointed by the department in consultation with the director of said regional branch. At least eight of the members of an advisory council shall be parents who reside in the region, and whose children are enrolled in a special education program; provided, however, that no more than two parents on each such advisory council shall be parents of children who are not in public school day programs.

Each member shall be appointed for a term of three years. No member may be appointed for more than two consecutive terms. Each advisory council shall advise the regional branch regarding all aspects of special education programs within the region and shall submit a written report annually on the quality and adequacy of such programs to the state advisory commission established under section one Q. In addition to its other powers and duties, the advisory council shall hear and transmit to said state advisory commission, complaints and suggestions of persons interested in special education in the region. Members of each advisory council shall be granted access to special education programs and to information about such programs, subject to restrictions established by the board of education regarding confidentiality, and shall be assisted in carrying out their duties by the regional branch of the division of special education. Members of the advisory councils shall be reimbursed by the commonwealth for expenses necessarily incurred in the performance of their duties.

Section 1Q. There shall be established in the department a state advisory commission for special education, hereinafter called the commission.

Each special education advisory council established pursuant to section one P shall elect two representatives to the commission, at least one of whom shall be a parent or guardian whose child is receiving special education.

The commissioners of the departments of mental health, public health and public welfare shall each appoint a representative to serve as ex officio members of the commission. Members of the commission shall be reimbursed for expenses which are necessarily incurred in the performance of their duties. The commission shall annually submit a report to the department evaluating the quality and adequacy of special education programs in the commonwealth and recommending improvements in those programs. The department shall implement the recommendations of the commission or shall state in a written reply to said commission the reasons why such recommendations can not or should not be implemented. In such circumstances, the bureau responsible for hearing complaints and conducting investigations in the division of special education pursuant to section one N shall attempt to resolve the disagreement informally; provided, however, if a settlement cannot be reached the state board of education shall conduct public hearings to investigate the bases for the disagreement and resolve any dispute between the department and the commission.

SECTION 3. The second sentence of section 35 of chapter 41 of the General Laws, as appearing in section 2 of chapter 143 of the acts of 1937, is hereby amended by inserting after the word "officers", in line 3, the following words:—; provided, however, reimbursements made to a city or town under section thirteen of chapter seventy-one B shall be made to the school committees of such cities and towns and shall be used for special education programs pursuant to said chapter seventy-one B without further appropriation.

SECTION 4.   Section 53 of chapter 44 of the General Laws is hereby amended by striking out the first sentence and inserting in place thereof the following sentence;—All moneys received by any city, town or district officer or department, except as otherwise provided by section thirteen of chapter seventy-one B and by special acts and except fees provided for by statute, shall be paid by such officers or department upon their receipt into the city, town or district treasury.

SECTION 5.   Subsection (b) of section 18A of chapter 58 of the General Laws is hereby amended by striking out paragraph (3), as most recently amended by section 3 of chapter 1005 of the acts of 1971, and inserting in place thereof the following paragraph:—

(3) On or before November twentieth, the reimbursement for the special education programs required to be paid by the commonwealth under chapters seventy-one A and seventy-one B.

SECTION 6.   The third sentence of the second paragraph of section 7C of chapter 69 of the General Laws, as appearing in section 2 of chapter 403 of the acts of 1960, is hereby amended by striking out the words "of the mentally retarded", in line 5.

SECTION 7.   The third sentence of the second paragraph of section 7D of said chapter 69, as appearing in chapter 702 of the acts of 1963, is hereby amended by striking out the words "of the mentally retarded", in line 4.

SECTION 8.   Sections twenty-six to twenty-nine E, inclusive, and sections thirty-two to thirty-four, inclusive, of said chapter sixty-nine are hereby repealed.

SECTION 9.   Paragraph (c) of section 2 of chapter 70 of the General Laws, as most recently amended by section 6 of chapter 871 of the acts of 1970, is hereby further amended by striking out the words, "for special classes for the physically handicapped and the mentally retarded", in lines 4 and 5.

SECTION 10.   Sections forty-six to forty-six B, inclusive, sections forty-six D to forty-six F, inclusive, and sections forty-six H to forty-six M, inclusive, of chapter seventy-one of the General Laws are hereby repealed.

SECTION 11.   The General Laws is hereby amended by inserting after chapter 71A the following chapter.—

CHAPTER 71B

CHILDREN WITH SPECIAL NEEDS

Section 1.   The following words as used in this chapter shall, unless the context requires otherwise, have the following meanings: "Department", the department of education; "School age child", any person of ages three through twenty-one who has not attained a high school diploma or its equivalent; "School age child with special needs", a school age child who, because of temporary or more permanent adjustment difficulties or attributes arising from intellectual, sensory, emotional, or physical factors, cerebral dysfunctions, perceptual factors, or other specific learning disabilities or any combination thereof, is unable to progress effectively in a regular school program and requires special classes, instruction periods, or other special education services in order to successfully develop his individual educational potential; "Regular education", the school program and pupil assignment which normally leads to college preparatory or technical education or to a career; "Special education", educational programs and assignments, namely special classes, programs or services designed to develop the educational protential of children with special needs including but not limited to educational placements of children by school committees, the departments of public health, mental health, and youth services and the division of family and children's services in accordance with the regulations of the department of education; "School age child requiring special education", any child with special needs who requires special education as determined in accordance with the regulations set forth by the department.

Section 2. The department shall promulgate, in cooperation with the departments of mental health, public health and welfare, regulations regarding programs for children with special needs including but not limited to a definition of special needs; provided, however, that such definition shall emphasize a thorough narrative description of each child's developmental potential so as to minimize the possibility of stigmatization and to assure the maximum possible development of a child with special needs, and, provided further, that such definition shall be sufficiently flexible to include children with multiple special needs. Children receiving or requiring special education shall be entitled to participate in any of the following programs: (1) additional direct or indirect instruction consultation service, materials, equipment or aid provided children or their regular classroom teachers which directly benefits children requiring special education; (2) supplementary individual or small group instruction or treatment in conjunction with a regular classroom program; (3) integrated programs in which children are assigned to special resource classrooms but attend regular classes to the extent that they are able to function therein; (4) full-time special class teaching or treatment in a public school building; (5) teaching or treatment at home; (6) full-time teaching or treatment in a special day school or other day facility; (7) teaching or treatment at a hospital; (8)

teaching or treatment at a short or long term residential school; (9) occupational and pre-occupational training in conjunction with the regular occupational training program in a public school; (10) occupational and pre-occupational training in conjunction with full-time special class teaching in a public school building, at home, special day school or other day facility, hospital, or short or long-term residential school; (11) any combination or modification of programs (1) through (10) or other programs, services, treatments or experimental provisions which obtain the prior approval of the department.

Admission to such programs on the pre-school level at an earlier age than at which schooling is ordinarily provided shall be regulated by the department in conjunction with the departments of public health and mental health and shall be restricted to children with substantial disabilities who are judged by said departments to require such programming.

No child shall be assigned to a special education class unless it is first determined by an evaluation of the child's needs and the particular special education program that the child is likely to benefit from such program; periodically thereafter, and in no event less often than annually the child and his program shall be reevaluated to determine whether said child is benefiting from such program in accordance with the procedures set forth in section three. In the event that said program is not benefiting the child and that another program may benefit the child more, or said program has benefited the child sufficiently to permit reassignment, the child shall be reassigned, and in the event of consistent failure of a program to benefit children there assigned, the program shall be abolished or altered.

Section 3. In accordance with the regulations, guidelines, and directives of the department issued jointly with the departments of mental and public health and with assistance of the department, the school committee of every city, town or school district shall identify the school age children residing therein who have special needs, diagnose and evaluate the needs of such children, propose a special education program to meet those needs, provide or arrange for the provision of such special education program, maintain a record of such identification, diagnosis, proposal and program actually provided and make such reports as the department may require. Until proven otherwise every child shall be presumed to be appropriately assigned to a regular education program and presumed not to be a school age child with special needs or a school age child requiring special education.

No school committee shall refuse a school age child with special needs admission to or continued attendance in public school without the prior written approval of the department. No child who is so refused shall be denied an alternative form of education approved by the department, as provided for in section ten, through a tutoring program at home, through enrollment in an institution operated by a state agency or through any other program which is approved for the child by the department.

No child shall be placed in a special education program without prior consultation, evaluation, reevaluation, and consent as set forth and implemented by regulations promulgated by the department.

Within five days after the referral of a child enrolled in a regular education program by a school official, parent or guardian, judicial officer, social worker, family physician, or person having custody of the child for purposes of determining whether such child requires special education, the school committee shall notify the parents or guardians of such child in writing in the primary language of the home of such referral, the evaluation procedure to be followed, and the child's right to an independent evaluation at clinics or facilities approved by the department under regulations adopted jointly by the department and the departments of mental health and public health and the right to appeal from any evaluation, first to the department, and then to the courts.

Within thirty days after said notification the school committee shall provide an evaluation as hereinafter defined. Said evaluation shall include an assessment of the child's current educational status by a representative of the local school department, an assessment by a classroom teacher who has dealt with the child in the classroom, a complete medical assessment by a physician, an assessment by a psychologist, an assessment by a nurse, social worker, or a guidance or adjustment counselor of the general home situation and pertinent family history factors; and assessments by such specialists as may be required in accordance with the diagnosis including when necessary, but not limited to an assessment by a neurologist, an audiologist, an ophthalmologist, a specialist competent in speech, language and perceptual factors and a psychiatrist.

The department jointly with the departments of mental health and public health shall issue regulations to specify qualifications for persons assessing said child.

These departments through their joint regulations may define circumstances under which the requirement of any or all of these assessments may be waived so long as an evaluation appropriate to the needs of the child is provided.

Those persons assessing said child shall maintain a complete and specific record of diagnostic procedures attempted and their results, the conclusions reached, the suggested courses of special education and medical treatment best suited to the child's needs, and the specific benefits expected from such action. A suggested special education program may include family guidance or counseling services. When the suggested course of study is other than regular education those persons assessing said child shall present a method of monitoring the benefits of such special education and conditions that would indicate that the child should return to regular classes, and a comparison of expected outcomes in regular class placement.

If a child with special needs requires of a medical or psychological treatment as part of a special education program provided pursuant to this section, or if his parent or guardian requires social services related to the child's special needs, such treatment or services, or both, shall be made available, in accordance with regulations promulgated jointly by the departments of education, mental health, public health and public welfare in connection with the child's special education program. Reimbursement of the costs of such treatment or services or both shall be made according to the provisions of section thirteen.

Upon completion of said evaluation the child may obtain an independent evaluation from child evaluation clinics or facilities approved by the department jointly with the departments of mental health and public health or, at private expense, from any specialists.

The written record and clinical history from both the evaluation provided by the school committee and any independent evaluation, shall be made available to the parents, guardians, or persons with custody of the child. Separate instructions, limited to the information required for adequate care of the child, shall be distributed only to those persons directly concerned with the care of the child. Otherwise said records shall be confidential.

The department may hold hearings regarding said evaluation, said hearings to be held in accordance with the provisions of chapter thirty A. The parents, guardians, or persons with custody may refuse the education program suggested by the initial evaluation and request said hearing by the department into the evaluation of the child and the appropriate education program. At the conclusion of said hearing, with the advice and consultation of appropriate advisory councils established under section one P of chapter fifteen, the department may recommend alternative educational placements to the parents, guardians or persons with custody, and said parents, guardians and persons with custody may either consent to or reject such proposals. If rejected, and the program desired by the parents, guardian or person with custody is a regular education program, the department and the local school committee shall provide the child with the educational program chosen by the parent, guardian or persons with custody except where such placement would seriously endanger the health or safety of the child or substantially disrupt the program for other students. In such circumstances the local school committee may proceed to the superior court with jurisdiction over the residence of the child to make such showing. Said court upon such showing shall be authorized to place the child in an appropriate education program.

If the parents, guardians or person with custody reject the educational placements recommended by the department and desire a program other than a regular education program, the matter shall be referred to the state advisory commission on special education to be heard at its next meeting. The commission shall make a determination within thirty days of said meeting regarding the placement of the child. If the parents, guardians or person with custody reject this determination, they may proceed to the superior court with jurisdiction over the residence of the child and said court shall be authorized to order the placement of the child in an appropriate education program.

During the course of the evaluations, assessments, or hearings provided for above, a child shall be placed in a regular education program unless such placement endangers the health or safety of the child or substantially disrupts such education program for other children.

No parent or guardian of any child placed in a special education program shall be required to perform duties not required of a parent or guardian of a child in a regular school program.

Within ten months after placement of any child in a special education program, and at least annually thereafter the child's educational progress shall be evaluated as set forth above. If such evaluation suggests that the initial evaluation was in error or that a different program or medical treatment would now benefit the child more, appropriate reassignment or alteration in treatment shall be recommended to the parents, guardians or persons having custody of the child. If the evaluation of the special education program shows that said program does not benefit the child to the maximum extent feasible, then such child shall be reassigned.

Evaluations and assessments of children and special education programs shall remain confidential and be used solely for the administration of special education in the commonwealth, including, but not limited to, inspection by the department and regional and state advisory councils to insure that every special education program does benefit the children there assigned.

Section 4. The school committee of any city, town or school district may, to meet its obligations under section three, with the approval of the department enter into an agreement with any other school committee to jointly provide special education or, subject to the consent of the parent or guardian affected thereby and subject to constitutional limitations, may enter into an agreement with any public or private school, agency, or institution to provide the necessary special education within the city, town or school district.

In the case of an agreement between school committees to jointly provide special education, said agreement shall designate one city, town or school district as the operating agent. Funds received by such operating agent from other cities, towns or school districts or appropriated by such operating agent for the purposes of such agreement, in addition to gifts and grants shall be deposited with and held as a separate account by its treasurer. The school committee may apply said funds to the costs of programs operated pursuant to the agreement without further appropriation.

Section 5. Any school committee which provides or arranges for the provision of special education pursuant to the provisions of section three shall pay for such special education personnel, materials and equipment, tuition, room and board, transportation, rent and consultant services as are necessary for the provision of such special education.

A school committee which incurs costs or obligations as a result of section five of chapter one hundred and seventy-one B of the General Laws, inserted by section eleven of this act, shall include within its budget for its fiscal year which includes September first, nineteen hundred and seventy-three, and annually thereafter, an amount of money to comply with the provisions of said chapter. Said amount shall be added to the annual budget appropriation for school purposes in each city or town and shall be a portion of the amount necessary in such city or town for the support of public schools for the purposes of, and enforceable pursuant to, section thirty-four of chapter seventy-one, notwithstanding any general or special laws or charter provisions which limit the amount of money that may be appropriated in any city or town for school purposes.

Section 6. School committees shall annually report to the department, pursuant to regulations promulgated by the department, the assignment by sex, national origin, economic status, race and religion, of children by age level to special education classes and the distribution of children residing in the district by sex, national origin, economic status, race and religion of children by age level. Within any school district if in any special education program there is a pattern of assignment throughout the district on the basis of sex, national origin, economic status, race or religion of the students which is substantially disproportionate from the distribution, the department shall notify such school district of its prima facie denial of equal educational opportunities. The department shall hold public hearings to investigate into such prima facie denial, at which hearings the local school district must show that such disproportion is necessary to promote a compelling education interest of the children affected and of the commonwealth. If the local school district fails to make such showing, a denial of equal educational opportunities shall be declared by the department and it shall order said district to submit a plan to eliminate such denial to be effective for the school year immediately following such declaration and order. If in the view of the department the plan submitted is inadequate, or if implementation of said plan proves inadequate, the department may request the attorney general to proceed to the superior court for all necessary injunctive and other relief. If such prima facie denial has continued without elimination for a period of two consecutive years in any school district, any person residing in such school district may bring suit in the superior court of his residence to determine whether there is such adequate justification for the prima facie denial, and in the event there is not, to obtain the necessary and appropriate injunctive or other relief.

Section 7. No results of standardized or local tests of ability, aptitude, attitude, affect, achievement, or aspiration may be used exclusively in the selection of children for referral, diagnosis, or evaluation. Such tests must be approved by the department in accordance with regulations issued by the board to insure that they are as free as possible from cultural and linguistic bias or, wherever necessary, separately evaluated with reference to the linguistic and cultural groups to which the child belongs.

Section 8. If a school age child with special needs attends a school approved by the department within or without the city or town of residence of the parent or guardian, the school committee of the town where the child resides may be required by the department to provide transportation once each day including weekends where applicable to and from such school while the child is in attendance. The city or town providing transportation under this section shall be reimbursed according to the provisions of section thirteen.

Section 9. The department, after consultation with the departments of mental health and public health, shall define the circumstances in which school committees may be required to provide special classes, instruction periods or other special education programs for school age children with special needs and shall provide standards for class size, curriculum, personnel and other aspects of special education for such children.

Section 10. The department may, on an annual renewal basis, upon the request of the parents or guardians and the recommendations of a local school committee and a regional branch of the division of special education, and with the approval of the secretary of educational affairs refer children requiring special education to any institution within or without the commonwealth which offers curriculum, instruction and facilities which are appropriate to the child's needs and which are approved by the department under regulations prescribed by the departments of education, mental health and public health. The curriculum at such an institution must for approval be equivalent, insofar as the department deems feasible, to the curriculum for children of comparable age and ability in the public schools of the commonwealth.

Before acting on said request the department shall determine the nature and extent of a child's special needs, shall require the local school committee and regional advisory council to prepare and submit plans detailing the time needed to establish facilities adequate for children with special needs in the city, town or school district where the child resides, and shall ascertain whether adequate facilities and instruction programs are available or when adequate facilities can be made available in the city, town or school district where the child with special needs resides. Until adequate facilities can be made available, such child shall be placed in the most adequate program available as determined by the department. The department shall further define by regulation the circumstances in which it shall be directly responsible for the placement of children in such special education programs, and by standards available to the public determine the methods and order of such placements; provided, however, that no child shall be denied access to any program operated by the department of mental health, public health or public welfare to which in the judgment of the operating department the child should be admitted.

The expenses of the instruction and support actually rendered or furnished to such children with special needs, including their necessary travelling expenses, whether daily or otherwise, but not exceeding ordinary and reasonable compensation therefor, may be paid by the commonwealth; but the department shall issue regulations jointly with the departments of mental health, public health, youth services and public welfare defining the circumstances in which the commonwealth shall bear all or part of such cost, the circumstances in which school committees shall be required to bear part or all of such cost, and the circumstances in which a parent or guardian may be required to reimburse the commonwealth for part or all of such cost; provided, however, that in no event shall the cost to the school committee for placement under this section be less than the average per pupil cost for pupils of comparable age within the city, town or school district; and, provided further, that in determining the cost to the parent or guardian, if any, no charge shall be made for any educational cost but only for support and care. In determining the cost to the parent or guardian the department shall apply criteria which take into account relative ability to pay.

The department shall direct and supervise the education of all such children, and the commissioner of education shall state in his annual report their number, the cost of their instruction and support, the manner in which the money appropriated therefor has been expended, to what extent reimbursed and such other information as he deems important.

Nothing contained herein shall affect the continued authority of the departments of mental health and public health over all noneducational programs and all treatment for residents or patients in institutions under their control.

Section 11.   The department is hereby authorized to cooperate with cities and towns which establish recreation programs for school age children with special needs.

Such programs shall be under the direction and approval of the division of special education, and the department shall reimburse said cities and towns for one half of the cost thereof, including transportation of said children to and from the site of such program on each day said program is held. The department shall also fully reimburse a city or town in which said children are residents for the cost of transportation to and from recreation programs at any state facility whose recreation programs are approved by the department for the purposes of this section.

Section 12.   The department shall establish and maintain a school department for school-age children in each institution under the control of the departments of mental health, public health and youth services which provides support and care for resident children with special needs, acting jointly with the department which has control over the particular institution; provided, however, that appropriations for the administration of said school departments shall be administered by the department of education.

Each such school department shall be administered by a director, appointed jointly by the commissioner of education and the superintendent of said institution.

Each such school department shall have such staff as the department and the department which administers the institution involved deem appropriate.

Such school departments shall operate pursuant to regulations established jointly by the department and the department which administers said institution. Nothing contained herein shall affect the continued authority of departments operating such institutions over all non-educational programs and all treatment for residents or patients in institutions under their control.

The director and staff of such school departments shall be employees of the department of education, which shall assume the costs of all aspects of the educational programs in such departments. Said school departments may operate twelve months of the year. The salaries of school department personnel shall be paid at a rate at least equivalent to that of the average statewide public school salaries for comparable personnel employed in the public schools, as adjusted to account for the longer school year in the school departments. The total employee benefits accruing to such personnel in vacation, sick leave, tenure, and retirement benefits shall be similarly comparable to those of public school personnel, as adjusted to account for the longer school year in the school departments. Nothing contained herein shall operate to remove from employment any educational personnel already employed by any institution now under the administration of the department of mental health, public health or youth services, or to reduce their salaries or other employee benefits.

The per capita expenditure on education programs in such school departments shall be equivalent to or higher than the average expenditure for special education programs in the public schools of the commonwealth less the average transportation costs. Said average expenditure shall be computed annually by the department of education.

The city, town or regional school district in which each school-age child in any institution described hereinabove would normally be eligible to attend school shall pay to the commonwealth the costs of the education of said child in the school department of said institution in an amount determined according to the regulations issued under section ten; provided, however, that said payment for each such child shall not be less than its average per pupil cost for pupils of comparable age within the said city, town or school district. The amount due the commonwealth each year shall be deducted from the annual distribution to said city, town or school district pursuant to section eighteen A of chapter fifty-eight.

Section 13.   The cost of instruction, training and support, including the cost of special education personnel, materials and equipment, tuition, transportation, rent and consultant services, of the children in special classes, instruction periods or other programs provided under section three shall, for the amount by which such costs exceed the average per pupil expenditure of the city, town or school district for the education of children of comparable age, be reimbursed by the commonwealth to the city, town or school district as provided in section eighteen A of chapter fifty-eight; provided however, that the amount of such reimbursement for each special education pupil in the city, town or school district shall not exceed one hundred and ten per cent of the applicable state average expenditure for each special education pupil minus the state average expenditure per public school pupil. In determining the applicable state average expenditure for each special education pupil for the purposes of this section the department shall differentiate between types of programs on the basis of the amount of time a child requires special programs outside of the regular classroom to meet his particular needs and the ratio of personnel to pupils required for such programs. Such reimbursement shall be made only after approval and certification by the department that such expenditures are reasonable and the funds for such special education personnel, materials and equipment, tuition, transportation, rent and consultant services were actually expended and that such special education classes, instruction periods and other programs have met the standards and requirements prescribed by the department. The costs for each special education pupil shall be "reimbursable expenditures" within the meaning of chapter seventy, in an amount not to exceed the average per pupil expenditure for said city, town, or school district, and shall be reimbursed under said chapter.

The department shall reimburse a city or town in which a child resides who attends a clinical nursery school established under section twenty-seven of chapter nineteen or a child, who, because of insufficient classroom space in a clinical nursery school, attends a clinical nursery school, day care center or other institution for the care, education or treatment of retarded children conducted by an accredited school or college within the commonwealth, as provided in said section twenty-seven, or a retarded person who attends an educational, habilitational or day care program or facility of the department of mental health, as provided under section twenty-eight of said chapter nineteen, by paying one half of the cost of the transportation of each such child and the full cost of each such adult to and from such educational, habilitational or day care program or facility, as the case may be, one each day said school is in session.

Any reimbursements made to cities and towns under this section shall be made to the school committees of such cities and towns and shall be applied to the costs of programs provided for under this chapter without further appropriation.

Section 14. The state treasurer shall annually, on or before November twentieth, pay, under paragraph (3) of subsection (b) of section eighteen A of chapter fifty-eight, to any city or town or regional school district such sums as may be certified by the commissioner of education on account of special equipment purchased, leased and maintained or of classes or special instruction periods conducted as provided in section two.

SECTION 12. The first sentence of section 1 of chapter 76 of the General Laws, as amended by chapter 400 of the acts of 1950, is hereby further amended by inserting in line 22 after the word, "impracticable," the words, "subject to the provisions of section three of chapter seventy-one B".

SECTION 13. Said chapter 76 is hereby amended by striking out section 11 and inserting in place thereof the following section:—

Section 11. Any city or town which provides instruction to any child who is a resident of an institution and who was not theretofore a resident of such city or town may recover from the commonwealth the school expense incurred by reason of the school attendance of such child to be determined jointly by the school committee of such city or town and the department of education or, in case of the disagreement, by the probate court. The amount recoverable by a city or town under this section shall be limited to the annual per pupil cost of education as determined under section seven and no costs shall be reimbursed under this section which are reimbursable under section thirteen of chapter seventy-one B.

SECTION 14. The definition of "approved school projects" in section 5 of chapter 645 of the acts of 1948 is hereby amended by inserting after the second sentence the following sentence:—No school construction project shall be an approved school project unless and until the school building assistance bureau and the division of special education in the department of education are satisfied that adequate provisions have been made for children with special needs as defined in section one of chapter seventy-one B of the General Laws.

SECTION 15. The secretaries of the executive offices of human services and education shall jointly submit an annual report to the governor and the general court evaluating the success with which the departments under their administration have cooperated in the implementation of this act together with any recommendations for improving the ability of the commonwealth to meet the needs of children with special needs.

SECTION 16. A child who is in a special education program as of the effective date of this act shall be presumed to be appropriately assigned to said program until an evaluation pursuant to the provisions of section three of chapter seventy-one B of the General

Laws, inserted by section eleven of this act, indicates that another program would benefit said child more.

SECTION 17. ` No child with special needs in a special education program on the effective date of this act shall be removed from said program he is in without the written consent of the parents, guardians, or persons with custody of said child.

SECTION 18. A school committee shall not be responsible for more than the average per pupil cost for pupils of comparable age within the respective city, town or school district as its share of the cost of continuing placement for those children with special needs enrolled in an institution with his tuition paid by the commonwealth as of the effective date of this act.

SECTION 19. Departments issuing regulations pursuant to chapter seventy-one B of the General Laws, inserted by section eleven of this act, shall make such regulations available at least six months prior to the effective date of the act for review by a committee appointed by the board of education for such purpose. Said committee shall be representative of the several types of institutions now serving children with special needs, both public and private, and shall include members experienced in providing educational services to the several existing categories of special needs. Said committee shall further include members who are parents of children with special needs, both in public programs and private programs, members who are regular classroom teachers, members who are teachers primarily of children with special needs and members representing any other groups directly affected by this act or having expertise in the implementation of programs for children with special needs. Said committee shall include for each statutory category of children with special needs on the effective date of this act at least one member knowledgeable and experienced in working with such category of children.

SECTION 20. The members of a regional special education advisory council, established by section two of this act, first created shall consist of five members appointed for a one year term, five members appointed for a two year term, and six members appointed for a three year term.

SECTION 21. The amount reimbursed to a city, town or school district under section thirteen of chapter seventy-one B of the General Laws, inserted by section eleven of this act, combined with reimbursements for special education programs under chapter seventy of the General Laws shall not be less than reimbursements for special education programs received for the fiscal year nineteen hundred and seventy-four, until and unless said city, town or school districts qualifies for a lesser amount after September first, nineteen hundred and seventy-nine.

SECTION 22.   The provisions of this act are severable and if any provision shall be held unconstitutional by any court of competent jurisdiction, the decisions of such court shall not affect or impair any of the remaining provisions.

SECTION 23.   This act shall take effect on September first, nineteen hundred and seventy-four.

Approved July 17, 1972.

Notes

Chapter 1: The Shaping of a Special-Educator

1. An associate at London University is required to do graduate coursework, conduct a research project, and write a thesis. See John Henderson, "An Investigation of Psychological Services for Children" on file at the Institute of Education, London University, England, June 1972.

2. Kent County Council is the organization for the County of Kent, England, that hires all psychologists for the state schools. It hires foreigners by special permit. Queen Elizabeth's Hospital, London, is a children's hospital. Off Centre, for adolescent counseling, was funded by the Inner London Education Authority.

3. "Report of the Committee of Enquiry into the Education of Handicapped Children and Young People" (Chairman, H. M. Warnock) Her Majesty's Stationery Office, May 1978.

4. Elizabeth M. Anderson, "Making Ordinary Schools Special," College of Special Education (85 Newman Street, London, W.I.), London University, 1971.

Chapter 2: Launching a New Program

1. The Office for Children was created by the Massachusetts Legislature in July 1972 and began statewide operations in January 1973.

2. Drs. Harold Kaplan, Alfred Freedman, and Benjamin Sadock, comps., *Comprehensive Textbook of Psychiatry,* 3rd ed. (Baltimore/London: Williams and Wilkins, 1980), 1:200–201. Hyperactivity is defined as follows: "Syndrome in children first described by Bradley, 1937. The hyperkinetic syndrome in children is characterized by attention weaknesses, distractibility, overactivity, irritability, impulsiveness, low frustration tolerance and poor school performance."

3. Ritalin, the trade name for methylphidate, is useful when the child's signs and symptoms suggest a central processing disorder particularly with attention deficits and hyperkinesis.

4. Public Law 89-313, a federal law, was enacted to offer incentives to

school systems to develop their own programs for institutionalized children, so returning them to the less restrictive setting; in the meantime, moneys varied from year to year from between $700 and $900 per year per child for as long as the child remained on the special-education log.

5. Rossmiller, Hale, and Frohreich in *Special Education News,* published by the Education Division of Huntley Publishing Company, P.O. Box 402, Northfield, Illinois, 60093.

6. Ronald W. Conley, *The Economics of Mental Retardation* (Baltimore: Johns Hopkins, 1973).

Chapter 3: The Team Approach

1. Job description prepared by John V. Henderson, 1976.

2. The material on the Structural Learning Program has been written by Gayle Macklem. Gayle Macklem, School Psychologist, Manchester, Ma., author of article on Structured Learning Program, "A Place for Everyone," *Academic Therapy* 20, no. 2 (November 1984).

3. D. J. Johnson, and H. R. Myklebust, *Learning Disabilities: Educational Principles and Practices* (New York: Grune and Stratton, 1967).

4. John Curtis Gowan, "The Use of Developmental Stage Theory in Helping Gifted Children Be Creative," *Gifted Child Quarterly* 24, no. 1, 1980.

5. Lawrence Kohlberg, "The Cognitive Development Approach to Moral Education," *Phi Delta Kappa* (June 1975).

6. Clifford Swenson, "Ego Development and A General Model for Counseling and Psychotherapy," *The Personnel and Guidance Journal* 58, no. 5 (January 1980).

7. Robert Kegan, "Making Meaning: The Constructive-Developmental Approach to Personnel and Practice," *The Personnel and Guidance Journal* 58, no. 5 (January 1980).

8. D. Elkind, "Child Development and Counseling," *The Personnel and Guidance Journal,* 58, no. 5 (January 1980).

9. Lawrence Kohlberg 1975.

10. Jane Loevinger and Ruth Wessler, *Measuring Ego Development* (San Francisco: Jossey-Bass, 1978).

11. Robert Kegan 1980.

12. D. Elkind 1980.

13. Lawrence Kohlberg 1975.

14. R. B. Selman and A. P. Selman, "Children's Ideas About Friendship: A New Theory," *Psychology Today* (October 1978).

15. Dan Jacaquette, "Developing Conceptions of Peer-Group Relations from Childhood through Adolescence." Paper presented at the 1976 Convention of the Eastern Psychological Association.

16. Jane Loevinger, *Ego Development: Conceptions and Theories* (San Francisco: Jossey-Bass, 1977).

17. E. W. Cooney and R. L. Selman, "Children's Used Social Concep-

tions: Toward a Dynamic Model of Social Cognition," *The Personnel and Guidance Journal* 58, no. 5 (January 1980); and Clifford Swenson 1980.

18. Robert Kegan 1980.

19. *Piaget's Theory of Intellectual Development*, ed. Herbert Ginsburg and Sylvia Opper (Englewood Cliffs, N.J.: Prentice-Hall, 1969).

20. E. H. Erikson, *Childhood and Society*, 2nd ed. (New York/London: W. W. Norton & Co., 1964).

21. Lawrence Kohlberg 1975.

22. W. N. Dember, "The New Look in Motivation," *American Scientist* 53, 1965 as reported in Loevinger 1977.

23. Loevinger 1977.

24. Clifford Swenson 1980.

25. Donald Merchenbaum in *Cognitive Behavior Modification Newsletter* no. 4 (January 1979).

26. Margaret Dewey, *Teaching Human Relations to Special Students* (Maine: J. Weston Walch, 1978).

27. The Adventure Counseling curriculum was developed in the summer of 1980 by the Department of Pupil Personnel Services, Hamilton-Wenham (Mass.) Public Schools. This program incorporates problem-solving type athletic activities designed to positively shape the attitude and behavior of special needs students.

28. Piagetian Attainment Kit by Donald Buck, Ph.D., Assistant Professor, University of Wisconsin, Copyright by Paul S. Amidon Associates Inc.

Chapter 4: The Massachusetts Human Service Systems

1. Acts and Resolves of the Great and General Court, Chapter 704 of the General Laws, Section 16.

2. Repealed. See now c. 17/14.

3. Abolished. See now Department of Youth Services, c. 18A/1 et seq.

4. St. 1978, c. 552, amended this section in conformity with establishment by the act of the Department of Social Services within the Executive Office of Human Services. See G.L. c. 18B/1 and the note thereunder.

5. Summary statement in *Guide to Human Services for School Managers*, prepared by Massachusetts Department of Education and the Executive Office of Human Services, 1978.

Chapter 6: The Special-Education Appeals Process

1. 20 U.S.C. sections 1401-22 (1975).

2. See 20 U.S.C. section 1415 (1975) (specifying procedural safeguards). Included among the required procedures are an opportunity for the parent or guardian to examine all relevant records and to obtain an independent evaluation of the child, procedures to protect the rights of a

handicapped child whose parents are unknown, prior written notice whenever a public school proposes to initiate a change in a child's placement, and procedures designed to fully inform the parents of their rights in their native language. 20 U.S.C. sections 1415 (b)(1)(A)–(D); see also 34 C.F.R. sections 300.502–.505 (1981).

3. 20 U.S.C. section 1415 (b) (2).

4. See, e.g., 34 C.F.R. sections 300.532–.533 (1981); 34 C.F.R. sections 300.343–.346 (1981).

5. See 34 C.F.R. section 300.504 (b) (ii) (1981) (requiring parental consent before placement of handicapped child in special-education program).

6. 20 U.S.C. section 1415 (b) (1) (D); 34 C.F.R. section 300.506 (1981).

7. 34 C.F.R. section 300.506 (a) (1981).

8. Compare New York Education Law sections 4401, et seq. (McKinney) (providing two-tiered approach of local and state administrative review), with Mass. Gen Laws Ann. ch. 71B, section 3 (West Supp. 1981) (state agency conducts hearings concerning placement of special-needs children).

9. 20 U.S.C. section 1415 (b) (2); 34 C.F.R. section 300.507 (1981).

10. 34 C.F.R. section 300.506 (c) (1981).

11. See 34 C.F.R. section 300.507 (1981).

12. 20 U.S.C. section 1415 (d); 34 C.F.R. section 300.508 (a) (1)–(3) (1981).

13. Similar to the federal Administrative Procedure Act, 5 U.S.C. sections 551 et seq.; state laws define rules for the conduct of agency hearings and typically permit that agencies need not observe the rules of evidence observed by the courts. E.g., Mass. Gen. Laws Ann. ch. 30A, section 11 (2) (West, 1979).

14. E.g., Mass. Gen. Laws Ann. ch. 30A, section (11) (2) (West, 1979).

15. See 20 U.S.C. section 1412 (1): states must enact policies which assure all handicapped children the right to a free appropriate public education.

16. Compare Case No. 5A-80, 3 Educ. Hand. L. Rep. 502:172, 173 (Calif., Mar. 27, 1980) (burden on school district to prove that its placement is appropriate) and Case No. 1980-28, 3 Educ. Hand. L. Rep. 502:203, 204 (Ga., Nov. 13, 1980) (local school system met burden of establishing that it could provide appropriate educational placement) with Case No. 158, 3 Educ. Hand. L. Rep. 502:111, 112 (Calif., July 18, 1980) (where parents requested extended summer program, burden was on them to prove that child would regress without such program) and Case No. 149, 3 Educ. Hand. L. Rep. 502:191, 193 (Pa., Aug. 13, 1980) (where local agency introduced substantial evidence in support of its proposed program, burden shifted to parents to prove school's program inappropriate).

17. See 20 U.S.C. section 1412 (B) (5) (requiring that to maximum extent appropriate handicapped children be educated with nonhandicapped children); see also 34 C.F.R. section 300.550 (b) (1) (1981). See generally *Springdale Sch. Dist.* v. *Grace*, 656 F. 2d 300 (8th Cir., 1981); *Kruelle* v. *New Castle County Sch. Dist.*, 642 F. 2d 687 (3d Cir., 1981).

18. See, e.g., 603 C.M.R. section 28.403.1 (1981).

19. See 20 U.S.C. section 1415 (d) (4); 34 C.F.R. section 300.508 (a) (5) (1981); see also 34 C.F.R. section 300.512 (1981) (outlining timelines in special education appeals).

20. See, e.g., *Mass Gen. Laws Ann.* ch. 30A, section 11(8) (West, 1979).

21. 20 U.S.C. section 1415 (d) (3)–(4); 34 C.F.R. section 300.508 (a) (4)–(5) (1981).

22. 20 U.S.C. section 1415 (e) (1); 34 C.F.R. section 300.509 (1981).

23. See text accompanying note 8 above (under two-tiered approach parties to hearing entitled to administrative review by both local and state agencies).

24. 20 U.S.C. section 1415 (c); 34 C.F.R. section 300.510 (a) (1981).

25. 20 U.S.C. section 1415 (e) (2); 34 C.F.R. section 300.511 (1981).

26. See *Burlington* v. *Department of Educ.*, 655 F. 2d 438, 431 (1st Circ., 1981) (when invoked, federal specification for review controls over inconsistent provisions of state law); accord, *Vogel* v. *School Bd. of Montrose*, 491 F. Supp. 989 (W.D. Mo., 1980).

27. E.g., *Kruelle* v. *New Castle County Sch. Dist.*, 642 F. 2d 687, 692 and nn. 16–17 (3d Cir., 1981); *Abrahamson* v. *Hershman*, C. A. No. 80-2513-K (D. Mass., Jan. 22, 1982) slip op. at 8; *Ladson* v. *Board of Educ. of D.C.*, 3 *Educ. Hand. L. Rep.* 551:188, 189 n. 4 (D.D.C., March 12, 1979).

28. See 20 U.S.C. section 1415 (e) (2).

29. See *Abrahamson* v. *Hershman*, C.A. No. 80-2513-K (D. Mass., Jan. 22, 1982) slip op. at 8; *Laura M.* v. *Special Sch. Dist. No. 1*, 3 *Educ. Hand. L. Rep.* 552:152, 155 (D. Minn., Jan. 21, 1980).

30. See *Kruelle* v. *New Castle County Sch. Dist.* 642 F. 2d 687, 692 and nn. 16–17 (3d Cir., 1981); *Abrahamson* v. *Hershman*, No. 80-2513 (D. Mass., Jan 22, 1982), slip op. at 8.

31. Cf. 1972 Mass. Acts. ch. 766, Preamble (promulgation of state special-education statute stemmed, in part, from past inadequacies in parent involvement); see also Senate Floor Debate (June 18, 1975), 121st Cong., Rec. S10955, S10970 (parent participation in placement process designed as cooperative effort).

Chapter 7: Issues in Special-Education Law

1. See, e.g., *Stemple* v. *Board of Educ. of Prince George's County*, 623 F. 2d 893, 894 (4th Cir., 1980), cert. denied, 450 U.S. 911 (1981); *Norris* v. *Massachusetts Dept. of Educ.*, No. 80-1527, slip op. at 13 (D.

Mass., Oct. 9, 1981); *Foster* v. *D.C. Bd. of Educ.*, 523 F. Supp. 1142, 1143 (D. D.C., 1981); *Monahan* v. *Nebraska*, 491 F. Supp. 1074, 1080 (D. Neb., 1980).

2. As a rule, questions of financial responsibility are always a proper subject for administrative or judicial review. See 20 U.S.C. section 1415 (b) (1) (E); 34 C.F.R. section 300.506 (a) (1981).

3. E.g., *Monahan* v. *Nebraska*, 645 F. 2d 592, 596 (8th Cir., 1981); *Stemple* v. *Board of Educ. of Prince George's County*, 623 F. 2d 893, 897–98 (4th Cir., 1980), cert. denied, 450 U.S. 911 (1981); *Foster* v. *D.C. Bd. of Educ.*, 523 F. Supp. 1142, 1146 (D.D.C., 1981); *Zvi D.* v. *Ambach*, 520 F. Supp. 196, 202–03 (E.D. N.Y., 1981).

4. E.g., *Blomstrom* v. *Department of Educ.*, No. 80-2577, slip op. at 7–9 (D. Mass., Feb. 12, 1982); *Amherst-Pelham Regional Sch. Comm.* v. *Department of Educ.*, 367 Mass. 480, 492, 381 N.E. 2d 922, 930–31 (1978); see also 603 C.M.R. section 28.504(f) (1981900) (permitting retroactive reimbursement for unilateral placements that administrative agency determines to be appropriate).

5. 20 U.S.C. section 1415 (e) (3); see also 34 C.F.R. section 300.513 (a) (1981).

6. E.g., *Stemple* v. *Board of Educ. of Prince George's County*, 623 F. 2d 893, 897 (4th Cir., 1980), cert. denied, 450 U.S. 911 (1981); *Monahan* v. *Nebraska*, 491 F. Supp. 1074, 1088–89 (D. Neb., 1980), aff'd, 645 F. 2d 592 (8th Cir., 1981); *Gagnon* v. *Massachusetts Dep't of Educ.*, No. 80-12229. slip op. at 3–4 (Mass. Super. Ct., Oct. 19, 1981) (granting stay of execution), vacated, No. 81-0419, slip op. (Mass. App., Dec. 24, 1981).

7. *Stemple* v. *Board of Educ. of Prince George's County*, 623 F. 2d 893, 897 (4th Cir. 1980), cert. denied, 450 U.S. 911 (1981).

8. Id. at 898.

9. E.g., *Blomstrom* v. *Department of Educ.*, No. 80-2577, slip op. at 7–9 (D. Mass., Feb. 12, 1982); *Amherst-Pelham Regional Sch. Comm.* v. *Department of Educ.*, 367 Mass. 480, 492, 381 N.E. 2d 922, 930–31 (1978).

10. *Amherst-Pelham Regional Sch. Comm.* v. *Department of Educ.*, 367 Mass. 480, 492, 381 N.E. 2d 922, 930–31 (1978).

11. *Fitzgerald* v. *Anrig*, No. 81-1849, slip op. (D. Mass., Dec. 21, 1981).

12. *Anderson* v. *Thompson*, 658 F. 2d 1209, 1216 (9th Cir., 1981).

13. Significantly, the U.S. Supreme Court denied a petition to review the decision of the circuit court in *Stemple* v. *Board of Educ. of Prince George's County*, 623 F. 2d 893 (4th Cir., 1980), cert. denied, 450 U.S. 911 (1981). Consequently, as one federal district court has noted, "until the statute is clarified by Congress or construed definitively by the Supreme Court, conflicts in interpretation will continue." *Blomstrom* v. *Department of Educ.*, No. 80-2577, slip op. at 6 n–5 (D. Mass., Feb. 12, 1982).

14. *Blomstrom* v. *Department of Educ.*, No. 80-2577, slip op. at 5 (D. Mass., Feb. 12, 1982); see also *Anderson* v. *Thompson*, 658 F. 2d 1209, 1212, 121 (9th Cir., 1981) (parents have right to move children to private schools, and retroactive reimbursement is allowable in certain circumstances).

15. E.g., *Anderson* v. *Thompson*, 658 F. 2d 1209, 1212 (9th Cir., 1981); *Blomstrom* v. *Department of Educ.*, No. 80-2577, slip op. at 8 (D. Mass., Feb. 12, 1982).

16. 20 U.S.C. section 1401 (17); 34 C.F.R. section 300-13 (a) (1981).

17. See 20 U.S.C. section 1401 (17). See generally *Druelle* v. *New Castle County Sch. Dist.*, 642 F. 2d 687, 693–94 (3d Cir., 1981) (discussing required nexus between educational needs and provision of related services).

18. See *Tatro* v. *Texas*, 481 F. Supp. 1224, 1227 (N.D. Tex., 1979).

19. E.g., *Kruelle* v. *New Castle County Sch. Dist.*, 642 F. 2d 687, 693 (3d Cir., 1981); *North* v. *D.C. Bd. of Educ.*, 471 F. Supp. 136, 141 (D.D.C., 1979); cf. *Battle* v. *Pennsylvania*, 629 F. 2d 269, 275 (3d Cir., 1980) (for severely handicapped children, education begins at most fundamental level of learning daily self-help skills).

20. *Kruelle* v. *New Castle County School Dist.*, 642 F. 2d 687, 693 (3d Cir., 1981).

21. See *Tatro* v. *Texas*, 625 F. 2d 557, 560–62 (5th Cir., 1980) (provisions of clean-intermittent-catheterization found to be related service because child could not even be in classroom without such service); accord, *Tokarcik* v. *Forrest Hills Sch. Dist.*, Nos. 80-2844/2845, 3 *Educ. Hand. L. Rep.* 552:513, 525–28 (3d Cir., 1981) (clean-intermittent-catheterization); *Hairston* v. *Drosick*, 423 F. Supp. 180, 184 (D. W. Va., 1976) (catheterization).

22. E.g., *Papacoda* v. *Connecticut*, No. 80-630, 3 *Educ. Hand. L. Rep.*, 552:595, 497–98 (D. Conn., 1981); *In re Claudia K.*, No. 80-280, 3 *Educ. Hand. L. Rep.* 552:501, 502 (Ill. Cir. Ct., 1981); *In re "A" Family*, No. 14815, 3 *Educ. Hand. L. Rep.*, 551:345, 349–51 (Mont., 1979).

23. See Akin, Black, Guarino, Klebanoff, and Rosenfield, Psychotherapy as a "Related Service," *Educ. Hand. L. Rep.*, AC 15, AC 35 (Nov. 13, 1981).

24. Cf. *Blomstrom* v. *Department of Educ.*, No. 80-2577, slip op. at 10 (D. Mass., Feb. 12, 1982) (parents are party normally vested with authority to make decisions regarding education of their children).

25. See *Goss* v. *Lopez*, 419 U.S. 565, 574–84 (1975) (discussing minimum due-process guarantees afforded before suspension or expulsion of public school students).

26. Id. at 584.

27. Id.; see *Dillon* v. *Pulaski County Special School District*, 468 F. Supp. 54 (E.D. Ark., 1978) (conferring upon student or student's counsel right to confront accuser and cross-examine witnesses).

28. *Stuart* v. *Nappi*, 443 F. Supp. 1235, 1243 (D. Conn., 1978); *accord, S-1* v. *Turlington*, 635 F. 2d 342 (5th Cir., 1981); *Doe* v. *Koger*, 480 F. Supp. 225 (N.D. Ind., 1979).

29. See *Stanley* v. *School Administrative Unit #4*, No. 80-9, 3 *Educ. Hand. L. Rep.* 552:390, 394-95 (D. N.H., 1980); *Mrs. A. J.* v. *Special School Dist. #1*, 478 F. Supp. 418, 432 n. 13 (D. Minn., 1979); *Stuart* v. *Nappi*, 443 F. Supp. 1235, 1242 (D. Conn., 1978).

30. See 20 U.S.C. section 1415, 34 C.F.R. sections 300.500-.534 (1981) (procedural safeguards).

31. See e.g., *S-1* v. *Turlington*, 635 F. 2d 342 (5th Cir., 1981); *Blue* v. *New Haven Bd. of Educ.*, No. 81-41, 3 *Educ. Hand. L. Rep.*, 552:401 (D. Conn., 1981); *Mrs. A. J.* v. *Special School Dist. #1*, 478 F. Supp. 418 (D. Minn., 1979).

32. E.g., *S-1* v. *Turlington*, 635 F. 2d 342, 347 (5th Cir., 1981); *Doe* v. *Koger*, 480 F. Supp. 225, 229 (N.D. Ind., 1979).

33. See letter from G. Jackson, Office for Civil Rights Region X Acting Regional Director, to Dr. D. Moberly, Supt. of Seattle School District #1 (March 3, 1981), reprinted in Stephens, "Procedural Due Process and the Discipline of Handicapped Students," *Inquiry and Analysis* at 5-6 (Nat. Sch. Bds. Assn., Nov. 1981).

34. Cf. *Mass. Gen. Laws Ann.*, ch. 71B, section 3 (West Supp., 1981) (even where school committee receives approval to remove handicapped child from classroom, school must arrange alternative form of special education). See generally 20 U.S.C. section 1412 (1) (states must enact policies to assure all handicapped children right to free appropriate public education).

35. 20 U.S.C. section 1401 (18); see also 34 C.F.R. section 300.4 (1981).

36. E.g., *Abrahamson* v. *Hershman*, No. 80-2513, slip op. at 8 (Jan. 22, 1982) (quoting *Battle* v. *Comm. of Pennsylvania*, 629 F. 2d 269, 278 (3d Cir., 1980).

37. Cf. *Kruelle* v. *New Castle County Sch. Dist.*, 642 F. 2d 687, 691 (3d Cir., 1981) (theoretically, scope and details of appropriate education are left primarily to state definition).

38. See *Battle* v. *Commonwealth of Pennsylvania*, 629 F. 2d 269, 279-81 (3d Cir., 1980) (although act leaves definition of appropriate education to states, courts have responsibility to determine whether federal act restricts state policies).

39. *Rowley* v. *Board of Educ. of Hendrick Hudson Cent. Sch. Dist.*, 483 F. Supp. 528, 534 (S.D.N.Y.), aff'd, 632 F. 2d 945 (2d Cir., 1980); *accord, Springdale Sch. Dist.* v. *Grace*, 656 F. 2d 300, 303 (8th Cir., 1981). See generally Note, "Enforcing the Right to an 'Appropriate' Education: The Education for All Handicapped Children Act of 1975," 92 *Harv. L. Rev.* 1103, 1125-27 (1979).

40. *Springdale School Dist.* v. *Grace,* 656 F. 2d 300, 303 (9th Cir., 1981).

41. *Bales* v. *Clarke,* 523 F. Supp. 1366, 1369–70 (E.D. Va., 1981).

42. See *Rowley* v. *Board of Educ. of Hendrick Hudson Cent. Sch. Dist.,* 483 F. Supp. 528, 534–36 (E.D.N.Y.), aff'd, 632 F. 2d 945 (2d Cir., 1980).

43. See *Springdale School Dist.* v. *Grace,* 645 F. 2d 300, 304 (9th Cir., 1981).

44. *Rowley* v. *Board of Educ. of Hendrick Hudson Cent. Sch. Dist.,* 632 F. 2d 945 (2d Cir., 1980), cert. granted, 50 U.S.L.W. 3334 (U.S., Nov. 3, 1981) (No. 80-1002).

Chapter 8: *Matthew* v. *A School System in Massachusetts*

1. R. Lejeune (1959) in *Mental Retardation, Nature, Cause, and Management,* George S. Baroff (Washington, D.C., Hemisphere Publishing, 1974).

2. S. A. and W. R. Canterwell (1960) in *Mental Retardation, Nature, and Management.*

3. H. Forssman and H. O. Akesson (1970) in *Mental Retardation, Nature, Cause, and Management.*

4. P.L. 766 Regulation, Massachusetts Department of Education, Sept. 1978, 502.4 *Substantially Separate Program.* Each school committee shall provide a program within this prototype to each child in need of special education for whom the individual education plan specifies such a program.

5. Jan. 25, 1984, BSEA Case #831160.

Chapter 9: A Close Look at the Law

1. Federal Funds for Special Education, 94-142 and 89-313, Massachusetts Department of Education, June 1979.

2. All figures are taken from State and Federal records and have been listed in round figures.

3. Supplement to Chapter 65A–74. School Funds and State Aid for Public Schools, 1978, Public Law, Chapter 70.

4. Frank H. Wood, ed., *Perspectives for a New Decade: Education's Responsibility for Seriously Disturbed and Behaviorally Disordered Children and Youth* (Reston, VA: Council for Exceptional Children, 1981).

5. H. D. Fredericks et al., *Teaching Research Motor Development Scale for Moderately and Severely Retarded Children* (Springfield, IL: C. C. Thomas, 1972).

6. *International Journal of Rehabilitation.*

7. David Braddock, *Opening Closed Doors: The Deinstitutionalization of Disabled Individuals* (Reston, VA: Council for Exceptional Children, 1977).

8. GAO, 1980.

9. L. J. Schweinhard and D. P. Weikart, *Young Children Grow Up: Effects of the Perry Preschool Program on Youths through Age 15* (Ypsilanti, MI: High Scope, 1980).

10. The most current reading of the Law is to be found at the State House Library, Boston, under the following heading: Annotated Laws of Massachusetts Cumulative Supplement to Chapters 65 A–74 as recompiled 1978, Issued March 1984.

11. Institute for Government Services, University of Massachusetts, Maurice A. Donahue, Director, *Cherry Sheet Manual,* June 1982.

Chapter 10: What Does the Future Hold?

1. Submitted as a position paper by the Special Education/Education Mutual (SEEM) Collaborative composed of the Massachusetts Towns of Wilmington, North Reading (home of the collaborative), Reading, Lynnfield, Stoneham, Woburn, and Winchester.

2. Chapter 750, a law enacted prior to P.L. 766 that provided for financial support for the handicapped children's programs funded in Chapter 750 were "grandfathered" in for as long as the need for service remained.

3. 502.3: Regular education program with less than 60 percent time out. 502.4: More than 60 percent time out.

Index

191